THE CHALLENGE OF STATEHOOD
Armenian Political Thinking
Since Independence

The Challenge of Statehood

Armenian Political Thinking
Since Independence

By

Gerard J. Libaridian

BLUE CRANE BOOKS
WATERTOWN, MASSACHUSETTS

THE CHALLENGE OF STATEHOOD
Armenian Political Thinkings Since Independence
By Gerard J. Libaridian

First Published in 1999 by

Blue Crane Books

P.O.Box 0291, Cambridge, MA 02238

First Edition

1   3   5   7   9   10   8   6   4   2

Cover design by Aramais Andonian

Book design, typography & electronic pagination by
Arrow Graphics, Inc. Watertown, Massachusetts

Printed in Canada

Library of Congress Cataloging-in-Publication Data

Libaridian, Gerard J., 1945–

The challenge of statehood : Armenian political thinking since
independence / Gerard J. Libaridian

p.   cm. — (Human rights & democracy)

ISBN 1-886434-10-7 (alk. paper)

1. Armenia (Republic)—Politics and government—1991–
2. Political culture—Armenia (Republic)
3. Nagorno-Karabakh Conflict, 1988–1994.
4. Armenia (Republic)—History—Autonomy and independence movements.

I. Title.   II. Series.

DK687.53.L53   1999

947.5608'6—dc21   99–20499

CIP

*To the memory of
Khachig "Harold" Khachigian
who believed that it was healthy
to think as a skeptic
but act as an optimist*

Acknowledgement

*The author gratefully acknowledges the support provided for this work
by the Fourth Millennium Society and many friends who,
nonetheless, bear no responsibility for its contents.*

CONTENTS

Preface

I started writing this book in order to share my thoughts on the meaning of events that took place in the Armenian world during the past decade and to identify what, in my view, is at stake. Most of the perspectives presented here can be traced back to articles and papers I have written, published, or presented since 1974.

Many of these perspectives were tested and crystallized as Armenians faced the challenge of statehood, and I had the rare opportunity to be a participant in, and not just an observer of, some of the events of the past decade. In the summer of 1990, the Armenian National Movement (ANM), founded by the Karabagh Committee, had won a majority of the seats in that moribund body and elected one of its leaders, Levon Ter-Petrossian, as its Chairman. Ter-Petrossian invited me to Yerevan to establish a Department of Research and Analysis in the Supreme Soviet.

I began work in Armenia in January 1991 for a six-month period. That task was accomplished by the time Ter-Petrossian was elected President of Armenia, and Armenia declared its independence in September 1991. The newly elected President asked me to remain a while longer as an adviser. In 1994 the same President designated me Senior Adviser and Secretary of the Security Council. He also gave me the rank of Ambassador and the position of Ambassador-at-Large to facilitate my work while on special missions outside the country. For the brief period from March 1993 to September 1994 I also served simultaneously, and quite reluctantly, as First Deputy Minister of Foreign Affairs.

During my seven years of work in Armenia, I was involved in policy formulation and negotiations with a number of countries and regional and international organizations, and I worked on some of the critical issues facing the new state, including two issues discussed in some detail in this volume: the Karabagh conflict and relations with Turkey. I resigned for personal reasons in September 1997 and returned to Cambridge, Massachusetts. The six months had lasted seven years.

To complete this background information, readers should also be aware that I grew up in a "Dashnaktsakan," or ARF (Armenian Revolutionary Federation), environment and was a member of that party for a long time. Its founders and history were sources of inspiration for me, as were many of its leaders, who founded and led the First Republic in 1918. While I would not have subscribed to all their actions and policies, these men stood apart, along with others of their generation, with the strength of their personalities and intellects. One of them, Simon Vratsian, the last Prime Minister of the First Republic, was one of my teachers and the principal of my school, the Palanjian Jemaran in Beirut. To have known him has always reinforced in me the belief in the possibility of a rebirth of independent statehood for Armenia. I resigned from the ARF in December 1988, when I concluded that the party's opposition to the popular movement in Armenia and Karabagh and to the leadership of that movement was neither accidental nor based on ignorance. While my travails with the ARF may explain the space it occupies in this study, I would like to believe that the reason for that anomaly is the anomalous position the ARF has occupied and still occupies in Armenian life.

Nonetheless, this is not a book of memoirs. As I told a friend while I was still working in Yerevan, one cannot do the work at hand and think of memoirs at the same time. One cannot make the mistakes one is bound to make while, at the same time, thinking of saving one's skin from history or from one's own judgment later on. Memoirs have also the disadvantage, if written honestly, of reflecting the truth, at least one person's truth, which can be very dull, very strange, and very fantastic, all at the same time. And the fantastic is always more entertaining, even more credible. The idealized is always more inspiring, though probably less useful. At the end, inspiration performs the same role as entertainment: to divert, but not to disturb. Analysis does not measure up to that expectation.

This is also not a history of the Nagorno Karabagh conflict, however central that is to the issues discussed here. Although it is already possible to write a credible history of the last decade, certain aspects will remain hidden for some time to come. Here, Karabagh is discussed in its role as a catalyst for political processes and debate, as well as the factor that has conditioned these processes. But how a party or personality sees the problem of Nagorno Karabagh and the solution, where in its worldview the problem fits, and what a party or individual does with the problem in the process are some of the questions raised in this volume.

The information in this book is based largely on material that is in the public domain. No sensational secrets are revealed! The novelty may be found in the assessment and analysis of otherwise well-known, though possibly obscured or forgotten, events and points of view, and in the context within which these are placed.

Furthermore, I have left out of this work the role that other states—near and far—have played in the political processes that have taken place in Armenia. My first defense for this omission is that, however significant other states may be, this work focuses on the way issues are understood and defined in Armenian political thinking. Second, Armenians must assume responsibility for their actions, positions, policies, and choices, for their failure to discern existing choices or, for that matter, for the inability to create options. Regardless of the role assigned to Armenia by other states in pursuit of their own interests, it is Armenians who must define their problems, agenda, vital interests, and strategies, and who must assess correctly those of others, whether "friends" or "enemies." It is up to Armenians to determine the arena and degree of commonalty or incompatibility of interests with another country or, for that matter, with any external force. To blame other countries when it is Armenians who have misread a situation may be good propaganda but it is bad history, bad leadership, and bad taste. The absence in this volume of a critique of policies and choices other states have made should not be interpreted as absolution for their share of responsibility in developments affecting Armenia and Armenians. The time for discussing the role of other states and their interaction with Armenian politics will come, too.

Finally, this book is neither a defense of policies of which I was part nor a response to the wealth of criticisms and attacks to which I was subjected prior to, during, or after my tenure of office in Armenia. Being criticized comes with the territory. Sometimes I got more than my share, particularly when what was written or said could not be defined, in any civil society, as criticism.

While I have tried to present objectively the position of other people, the book is biased; after all, it is my argument. I may be wrong or time may prove me wrong. Frankly, I hope I am, since what I have to say will comfort few and may disturb many readers. The analyses in this volume may also be seen as dangerous to many others. But perhaps one can take solace in the opinion expressed by Orson Welles: An idea that is not dangerous is not worth being called an idea.

I take responsibility for every opinion, idea, or analysis presented in this book. Times like these are perilous for people who want to make sense of events or to place them in a perspective. To discern, from among the relentless storm of tidbits of information and opinions, what is or will be significant may best be left to astrologers. Yet, whether policy maker or interested bystander, one is constantly called on to explain events, assess trends, and make judgments.

If the analyses and insights expressed here do help raise the right questions and foster debate, I will be more than gratified.

15 January 1999

THE CHALLENGE OF STATEHOOD
Armenian Political Thinking
Since Independence

Introduction

This book presents an argument in favor of rational discourse and informed debate as opposed to rhetoric or what a turn-of-the century socialist Armenian analyst, Yervand Balian, called "reflexive reactions." As such, it can be viewed as a sequel to my work written in 1989 and published in 1991, *Armenia at the Crossroads*. At that time for most Armenians in Armenia as elsewhere, independence was still a distant dream. It also had not occurred to me, and I suspect to anyone else, that I would end up working in Armenia on some of these same problems.

Ten years and plenty of history later, I leafed through that work to summarize the argument for this volume. I was struck by the fact that events since 1988 and particularly in 1998 have at least justified the questions raised there at the same time as they constituted an answer, though not a final one, to these questions:

> *Can Armenia be an independent state? To be more explicit, one can ask: Can Armenia achieve strategic and political viability as a sovereign state capable of defining and managing its own vital interests or does her survival mandate continuing as a vassal state of an imperial power in return for protection? . . . For too long the fear of neighbors has been the dominant factor in determining the answer to the question of Armenian independence. Engendered by a series of massacres and a genocide in the twentieth century, strengthened by the image of the brutal Turk, nurtured by the surviving specter of Pan-Turkism, internalized as the psychology of the victim and the colonized,*

manipulated by Armenia's self-appointed protectors, that fear has, in fact, distorted the perception of national interests, and has been confused with strategic thinking.

. . . The Genocide, its exploitation, and its denial by Turkey have paralyzed the collective psyche of the Armenian people. A nation of victims—at first of the violence, and subsequently of its denial—is incapable of sustaining a rational discourse. A nation cannot imagine the future if the only thing it can imagine the future bringing is further victimization. The denial of the future justifies the denial of the present and mandates an obsessive treatment of an overburdened past. . . .

. . . The national democratic movement . . . questioned the validity of the paradigm based on fear, raised doubts on the imminence of a Pan-Turkic danger, reestablished the right to determine a national agenda, and reintroduced rational discourse as the means to answer questions. (Armenia at the Crossroads, pp. 1–2)

. . . .

. . . We, in the Diaspora, should have the humility and courage to recognize that our institutions were not built to face the new, and bigger, challenges facing our nation. . . . Our political thinking has been meandering over the past seventy years, just as we, Diasporans, have been moving from country to country. . . . The time had come to reassess the issues of the past decades, to understand history and act in a way that makes real participation and real change possible. The time had come to distinguish between the real and the ritualistic. (Armenia at the Crossroads, Introduction and Postscript, p. 167)

Beginning with a debate in the Supreme Soviet of Armenia in 1989, the Armenian National Movement (ANM) gave one set of very clear answers to these questions: Armenia would have to overcome traditional thinking if it hoped to become a viable and independent state. This answer went counter to the conventional wisdom in Armenian political thought. The visceral opposition to the ANM and to Levon Ter-Petrossian, during their dominance of

Armenian politics and since their demise, is related directly to their position on this central issue. While there have been no final answers, the validity of the questions have been confirmed by the current debates, however truncated and demagogic these may be.

The monumental changes in Armenia, the Caucasus, and the world during the last decade have affected, directly or indirectly, the lives of all Armenians.

The USSR, of which Armenia was a constituent republic, was about to implode, but no government in the world and very few individuals expected that to happen. The USSR was still a super-power; all decisions, strategies, and calculations were made with the understanding that it was there to stay. The First Secretary of the Communist Party of the USSR and its actual leader, Mikhail Gorbachev, had "opened up" Soviet society with his *glasnost* (a degree of political openness) and *perestroika* (limited economic restructuring) in a last bid to save the USSR as a socialist system and as an empire. Even if other nations, especially in the West, did not want to see it, he knew the system was bankrupt politi-cally and economically.

In Armenia, as elsewhere in the USSR, the only political party functioning legally was the Communist Party. There were a vari-ety of nonrecognized groups and groupings; only Paruyr Hayrikian's National Self-Determination Union came close to constituting an opposition political party in Armenia, and he was exiled by Gorbachev.

Changes began in an otherwise quiet Soviet Armenia in the fall of 1987, when a group of environmentalists organized street demonstrations to protest an unsafe chemical industry polluting the city and the equally hazardous nuclear power plant of Medzamor near Yerevan, the capital. About five thousand citizens participated.

But it was on 20 February 1988, that a political earthquake struck Armenia and Armenian-populated Nagorno Karabagh, an Autonomous Region of Azerbaijan. On that date, the City Coun-cil of Stepanakert, capital of Nagorno Karabagh, adopted a reso-lution requesting that Moscow adjust the borders between Armenia and Azerbaijan to make Karabagh part of Armenia. This was a minor procedure within a state, the likes of which had been performed about a dozen times during Soviet rule. Both republics, Armenia and Azerbaijan, were part of a single state, the USSR, and the procedure would have constituted an internal administrative change with no international ramifications. The leaders of Karabagh also believed, or they were led to believe, that Moscow was sympathetic to such a request, if submitted formally and nudged by public display of Armenian popular support.

Karabagh's request was supported by massive rallies and demonstrations in Yerevan. Unusual in their character and sheer volume, these demonstrations received worldwide attention. They were, in fact, the first such movement by a people in what was then the Soviet bloc.

The reaction in Azerbaijan was strong and violent. For three days in late February and early March, Armenians living in the Azerbaijani industrial town of Sumgait were subjected to pogroms. The pogroms polarized public opinion in the two republics and politicized the issue. The inability of Soviet authorities to deal with and resolve the problem early increased the number of demonstrations. On occasion, the number of demonstrators reached a million, close to one-third of Armenia's population. Yet the crowds were always well-behaved and never violent. An initial "Karabagh Committee," made up largely of well-known Soviet Armenian intellectuals friendly to Moscow, was unable to diffuse or resolve the crisis. By May 1988 the original group was replaced by a more permanent Karabagh Committee, consisting of unknowns: Levon Ter-Petrossian, a philologist and historian; Vazgen Manukian and Babken Ararktsian, professors of Mathematics at Yerevan State University; Hambartzum Galstian, an ethnologist; Rafael Ghazarian, a physicist; Ashot Manucharian, a Communist Party Youth activist; Vano Siradeghian, a writer; as well as Davit Vardanian, Samvel Gevorkian, Samson Ghazarian, and Aleksan Hakobian. This group of people assumed the political and organizational leadership of the popular movement.

Unable to resolve the growing political conflict, Moscow arranged for what amounted to an exchange of populations between Armenia and Azerbaijan, though not involving Nagorno

Karabagh. About 170,000 ethnic Azeris were compelled to leave Armenia and were moved to Azerbaijan, while a still larger number of Armenians in Azerbaijan, close to 300,000, suffered the same fate and became refugees in Armenia, Russia, and some of the Central Asian republics. Yet neither this move, nor others taken by Moscow, resolved the problem of Karabagh. In fact, with every new step the conflict became bloodier and more complex.

The movement in Armenia, while remaining nonviolent, acquired more and more the character of a drive to democracy and independence.

In early December 1988 an earthquake devastated the north of Armenia and claimed more than twenty-five thousand lives. As the world focused on the tragedy, Soviet authorities in Moscow and Yerevan took the members of the Karabagh Committee into custody. They were imprisoned in Moscow. A second-tier leadership continued leading the Movement's activities, until the Committee members were released as a result of domestic and international pressure in June 1989. Soon after that, the Committee concluded that they must take charge of the Armenian state. The Karabagh Committee institutionalized its activities as the Armenian National Movement (ANM).

The ANM became the umbrella organization for a coalition of forces that contested the otherwise rubber-stamp Soviet Armenian Supreme Soviet, the legislative elections. In May and July 1989, the elections produced a victory for the ANM-led coalition. The ANM became the Government of Soviet Armenia in August 1990. Ter-Petrossian was elected President of the Presidium of the Supreme Soviet and promptly designated Vazgen Manukian as Prime Minister. Other members of the Karabagh Committee as well as second-tier leaders of the movement gradually took over the important positions in the Supreme Soviet and the Council of Ministers.

Within a few months, the Supreme Soviet passed fundamental laws changing the character of the Republic: A multiparty system, a free market economy, distribution of land to the peasants, freedom of religion and conscience, separation of Church and State, and others. By the end of 1990, Armenia was functioning as a sovereign state in domestic and economic matters, independent of Moscow, although it had yet to declare its independence. The ANM government also negotiated with Moscow the right of conscripts from Armenia to serve in units stationed on the territory of Armenia.

In April 1991 Soviet and Azerbaijani forces began the ethnic cleansing of Armenian-populated villages in the north of Nagorno Karabagh. The conflict was now militarized. Local resistance was minimal; villagers could not fight the army or armed forces with hunting guns. The population of 24 villages was deported, compelling Karabagh and Armenian authorities to organize groups of fighters that eventually constituted the core of the army of Karabagh.

The militarization of the conflict strained the ability of an ad hoc system of government to function adequately. While the Supreme Soviet retained legislative powers, executive power was shared by the prime minister and his cabinet and the Presidium of the Supreme Soviet. In the summer of 1991, the Supreme Soviet passed legislation authorizing a referendum on independence and creating the office of an executive President, with a clear separation of executive and legislative powers. In September 1991 an overwhelming majority of voters approved the referendum on independence. Armenia declared its independence.

While Vazgen Manukian thought he would be the one to assume the presidency, Levon Ter-Petrossian's popularity compelled Manukian to withdraw. Ter-Petrossian won the 1991 presidential elections with 83 percent of the popular vote. Paruyr Hayrikian, the dissident independentist who had served 17 years in Soviet prisons, came in second, with 7 percent of the vote. Other opposition candidates, including communists, the ARF, and independents, shared the balance. By the end of 1991 the USSR collapsed and the international community recognized the independence of the constituent republics of the USSR.

From September 1991 through 1994, two issues dominated the agenda of the republic: Karabagh and the economy. With the independence of Armenia and Azerbaijan, Karabagh became a conflict between two sovereign states, an international conflict by definition. The war with Azerbaijan intensified in 1992 and came to a halt in 1994. Armenian forces had not only kept Azerbaijanis out of most of Karabagh but had also occupied seven regions of that country surrounding Karabagh proper. Since 1988 the conflict had also produced new refugees and internally displaced people on both sides: close to 350,000 Armenians from Azerbaijan and Karabagh, almost 700,000 Azeris from Armenia, Karabagh, and surrounding Azerbaijani districts.

As for Armenia's economic crisis, the country shared with other former Soviet republics the consequences of the dissolution of the USSR, which, in turn, had collapsed at least partly because the empire's economy could no longer be sustained. The economic disaster was compounded by the collapse of old industrial relationships and markets. Armenia's economic crisis was also made worse by the blockades imposed by Azerbaijan in early 1991, long before the conflict was militarized, as a form of political pressure on Armenia to give up its support of Karabagh claims. The immediate results were a disruption of communications and transport and a paralyzing energy crisis. With the increasing successes of the Armenian forces, Turkey too supported the Azerbaijani pressure tactics. Except for a brief period between October 1992 and April 1993, Turkey refused to open its border and rail link with Armenia that could have provided alternative communications with the West and the Middle East.

Successive prime ministers struggled with the economy. Unable to receive raw materials, energy, and state subsidies from an economically stranded government or to export manufactured goods, many factories were shut down; exports lost their markets, and transport routes and could not compete with cheaper and higher quality products on the international markets; inflation and unemployment raged. At this same time, Russia changed its currency, compelling the Armenian government to expedite the introduction of the national currency. In the meantime, the middle class in Armenia had all but disappeared, poverty and emigration became widespread, and the reconstruction of the disaster zone was practically halted.

By 1994 economic reforms acquired a more systematic and planned character. The energy problem was resolved, at least temporarily, with the reopening of the nuclear plant. The economic slide was stopped, and some gains started appearing. But for the majority of citizens life remained a daily struggle.

The war had been all consuming. The 1994 cease-fire allowed some concentration in state and institution building. A Constitution, drafted by a special Commission over a three-year period, was adopted in 1995 by general referendum. Compared to the 1991 Law, the system provided by the new Constitution strengthened some of the powers of the President and weakened others. New elections for the National Assembly were held in the same year, as scheduled. Presidential elections too were held on schedule in 1996.

The results—a new National Assembly dominated by the Republic Bloc led by the ANM, and Ter-Petrossian reelected to a second term by a very thin majority—were contested by some of the opposition parties as well as by international observers as fraudulent.

The political consensus had disappeared as soon as some major items on the agenda (independence, basic laws on political and economic reforms) were resolved. Between 1991 and 1993 some members of the Karabagh Committee had left the ANM to organize their own parties and join the ranks of the opposition: Vazgen Manukian (the first Prime Minister) and Davit Vardanian (head of the Supreme Soviet's Permanent Committee on Foreign Relations) founded the National Democratic Union; Ashot Manucharian (Senior National Security Adviser to Ter-Petrossian until 1993) and Rafael Ghazarian (Chairman of the Supreme Soviet's Permanent Committee on Education and Science) later formed the Civic Union of Scientists and Industrialists (CUSCI); by the time he left his position as Mayor of Yerevan to become a businessman, Hambartzum Galstian had also drifted away from the ANM. Samson Ghazarian, a member of the Supreme Soviet, joined the ARF and then returned to the ANM fold.

Over time, second-tier leaders too started distancing themselves from the ANM and Ter-Petrossian. Hrand Bagratian, the longest-serving Prime Minister (1993–1996), founded his own party when he was replaced following the 1996 presidential elections; Edward Yegorian, Chairman of the National Assembly's Permanent Committee on State Building, and the day-to-day manager of the Committee to draft the Constitution, created his own "Hayrenik" or Fatherland faction in Parliament; and Davit Shahnazarian, an adviser to and special negotiator and, subsequently, Minister of Security under Ter-Petrossian, resigned his posts and became critical of the administration without joining any opposition party or forming one of his own.

By 1997 differences appeared within that part of the ANM that had been held together by the sheer personalities of the few leaders still working as a group: Ter-Petrossian as President of the Republic, Ararktsian as President of the National Assembly, Siradeghian as Minister of Interior (later as Mayor of Yerevan), and Samvel Gevorkian a member of the Supreme Soviet and subsequently Chairman of the Defense Committee of the National Assembly.

Ten years in positions of power and leadership had taken their toll on the leaders in different ways. The ANM had lost its top leadership to the legislative and executive branches. Particularly following the 1995 legislative elections, the governing party had become complacent, arrogant, self-confident, and careless, while the opposition had turned impatient. In addition, three years of the cease-fire had given an opportunity for new issues to surface and old ones to be redefined and restrategized. Parties had proliferated since 1991, and three Diasporan parties had established branches in Armenia as well.

At the end, the leadership of Karabagh, too, began to assert its own, more intransigent position on the resolution of the conflict. By the end of 1997, a weakened presidency and governing party could not withstand the pressures of those within the government who disagreed with Ter-Petrossian's attempt to find a compromise solution to the Karabagh problem. Ter-Petrossian's own prime minister and two key ministers repudiated his decision to accept a proposal by the international mediator as a basis of negotiations to transform the cease-fire in Karabagh into peace. A sufficient number of Republic Bloc deputies (none from the ANM) shifted their allegiance away from the President to deny him a majority in the National Assembly. Ter-Petrossian resigned in February 1998.

Robert Kocharian, once the leader of Karabagh whom Ter-Petrossian had invited to serve as Armenia's Prime Minister in 1997, assumed the function of Acting President according to the Constitution and was elected, as expected, President in second-round presidential elections in April 1998. The surprise was that of a large field of candidates, it was Karen Demirjian (the former First Secretary of the Soviet Armenian Communist Party governing Armenia when the Karabagh movement started) who came in second and had to be defeated in the second-round. Demirjian had stayed out of politics during the last decade and had no party base or organization when he decided to enter the race.

The legitimacy of that election too has been questioned by some opposition parties and international observers. Regardless, Kocharian's presidency marked the end of one era and the beginning of another in the life of the young republic.

The most daunting problem in this quest for a perspective on the last decade is finding the right questions to ask, the questions that might allow one to deal with the seemingly endless antagonisms, conflicts, contradictions and, above all, paradoxes in Armenian political life. One needs to find questions that might help make sense of the changing political agendas, the issues that reappear under different names, the shifting cause célèbres, and the treacherous headlines. One needs questions that might help distinguish between, on the one hand, real differences between political parties, personalities, and policies; and, on the other, political maneuvers, theater, and diversion. One is left wondering whether "they" know what they are doing—or is it "we" who do not understand politics?

Two questions may serve that purpose. What is the purpose of an independent Armenia? And, How do we decide what is the right answer to the first question?

These questions may seem removed from day-to-day events. But once one attempts to see how different political parties and leaders answer these questions, one will see that they constitute the substance of the battles being fought in the political arena. Part of the problem has been the assumption that no one could question the necessity of independence; it is taken for granted that independence should be taken for granted. Closer analysis indicates that for some people, independence has a relative or conditional value.

The first question dealing with the purpose of independence is not new, because Armenia has not had independence for almost a millennium, except for the brief period of the First Republic, 1918–1920. But independence had been on the political agenda, in different ways, almost since the time it was lost in 1045 in historic Armenia and in 1375 in Cilicia. Now that Armenia has recovered its sovereignty, the challenge is finding answers (individually and collectively) to the following questions: Why did Armenians want independence? What do they do with it now that it is there? How do they keep it? Is there another goal or value for which they may be or should be willing to sacrifice it? What is the mission of any government of an independent Armenia? What can one legitimately and realistically expect from it? What is or should be the proper role of the Diaspora?

Beyond political phrases and partisan slogans thrown out in the normal course of the struggle for political power, underpinning the shifts and coalitions, it is possible to discern the answers of groups representing two different worldviews. The first group consists of the pragmatists, people who want to use the opportunity of statehood to return Armenia and Armenians to the fold of humanity as a "normal" people. The second group believes statehood should be used as a vehicle to achieve a "higher" purpose, quality, mission, or program.

That much has become clear during the past decade, and especially during the past few years. For many people in Armenia and in the Diaspora, the battle was between those who were labeled "pragmatic" and those who espoused some form of "national ideology" and considered the lack of such an ideology as the worst of crimes. This latter group mistakenly believed that only those with an ideology could have visions or programs.

The differences in worldviews are most clearly seen in the role assigned to the Nagorno Karabagh conflict in the thinking and approaches of various groups and parties. Karabagh is the issue that brings together foreign policy, security, domestic politics, and economy. Karabagh is the test of agendas and programs, of parties and personalities. It is both a source of inspiration and a cause for concern. It elevates, but it also makes Armenians vulnerable to manipulation from within and without. Karabagh dominates Armenian politics in Armenia, whether it is an articulated part of the debate or not; and Karabagh overshadows Diasporan politics.

For most Armenians, these two answers—based on pragmatism or national ideology—only complement each other, and sets of goals can be achieved in stages. Whether the differences between the two groups can be resolved by spreading the goals pursued by each group over a period of time in the life of the republic is difficult to ascertain. It is my assertion that, under the circumstances, the two represent more than a conflict of policies and personalities: these answers reflect opposing worldviews based on conflicting self-definitions, individually and as a nation. They project a difference of view on the "soul of the nation," to borrow a metaphor. Political battles and international conflicts are most difficult to resolve and most ferocious when political views and positions are vested with the inner identity of the combatants, when the partisans feel they are fighting for the essence of one's nation, religion, or ideology, in fact, for an unquestionably "higher" good or value.

When working in Armenia, I often met politicians and administrators at their request. I always found it useful to ask my interlocutor to answer some questions at the start of the meeting. One such question was: What is the problem you are trying to solve with the solution you will be offering or the proposal you will be making? I always prefaced my questions by reassuring my interlocutor that I was willing to listen and discuss issues all day, but in order for me to follow the presentation more intelligently, it was useful to have the answer to that question as a starting point.

This was quite a useful approach, particularly with people who tended to talk too much and whose prefaces tended to be longer than the text. For one thing, the answer to the question, if I was able to extract it, tended to cut short the preface and presentation, and it forced them to think clearly and to be direct. In some cases the presentation would fizzle out, once that simple question was answered.

That happened, for example, in 1993 when as First Deputy Minister of Foreign Affairs I was asked by the President to represent the administration's position on a bill that was about to be offered in one of the permanent committees of the National Assembly. The bill was being offered by a deputy whom I knew well, with whom I had had many informal discussions, and who happened to be an ARF member of Parliament. Before beginning a formal debate in the committee, the chairman had wisely determined that an informal discussion might be appropriate, since the bill called for the unilateral abrogation of the 1921 Treaty of Kars delineating the borders between Armenia and Turkey.

The deputy began his presentation with a long preface, to which I listened carefully. He was about to start his introduction, the history of the Treaty, when I interrupted him very gently and informed him that I happened to be a historian; furthermore, I had been an ARF member for many, many years and, therefore, I had some idea of what he was talking about. I reassured him that I had reserved all day for the committee meeting and we need not hurry but that I would appreciate the answer to one question: What is the problem he was trying to resolve with this bill? To facilitate his answer I offered a list of the problems the administration was trying to resolve: waging a successful war, ensuring essential supplies—such as grain and oil—to the people under blockade conditions, establishing state institutions, making as much of the economy functional as possible, and a few similar issues. These may be the wrong problems to address and we may not have the best answers, I added, but at least we know what problems we are trying to resolve. What was the problem he was addressing? And, had he thought that whatever the problem, it is possible that the solution he was offering might create more problems than it solved? Was it feasible, for example, that Turkey would continue recognizing the borders fixed by the treaty, if Armenia abrogates the treaty unilaterally without having negotiated a new one? And in case it did not, what were the chances that Armenia's tanks would reach Van before Turkey's tanks reached Yerevan? Would such a step help or hurt the war we already had on hand?

Although we continued talking for another hour, the meeting had ended effectively in about fifteen minutes, when the chairman asked the sponsor of the bill if he still insisted on introducing the proposed draft formally. A very thoughtful deputy said, "It appears that this topic requires more thinking."

Most Armenians, regardless of party, are reasonable people and will respond to reason when that is the basis of the debate.

If Armenia was at the crossroads in 1989–1990, another way of introducing this work is to ask these questions: Has Armenia already crossed the road and in what direction has it traveled? Has it already made choices that are irreversible?

The short answer is that between 1990 and 1997 under the leadership of the ANM, Armenia had moved in the direction of independence and normalcy but, in the absence of a resolution to the Nagorno Karabagh conflict, had not yet reached the other side. Levon Ter-Petrossian's resignation halted the march in that direction. The direction has not yet been repudiated. Still, supporters of the new President, Robert Kocharian, and others not so friendly to him, would like to reverse it completely and move in the opposite direction.

In other words, this book is an attempt to explain if and in what way the events of the past decade have altered issues or responses, and where do Armenia and Armenians stand after independence and a war, after the successes and failures of the past ten years? Have the ideas and ideals of 1990 shaped subsequent events? Have events compelled Armenians to think differently? How was independence accepted, when some had doubted the wisdom of the idea? How are Armenians dealing with victory when it runs counter to the psychology of the victim? How are political traditions faring? How are traditional institutions dealing with the challenge of statehood when so much was predicated on its absence? How is the traditional understanding of history affecting the Armenian view of statehood today and, in turn, how is statehood challenging the traditional view of history? How are the dominant themes of preservation of identity, unity, and genocide recognition faring in a world where the flag of an independent Armenia flies along side those of other states?

Chapter 1 provides an overview of the Armenian political landscape since the rise of the movement and the position of political actors regarding the major issues confronting Armenia during the decade. Chapter 2 discusses the resignation of President Levon Ter-Petrossian as an event significant for understanding the relationship between the problem of Karabagh and the choices that must be made between the two kinds of answers, pragmatism and national ideologies. Chapter 3 details the position of political parties and leaders on the resolution of the conflict and the role the conflict is assigned in their political program and worldview. Chapter 4 covers the important themes of Genocide recognition, unity, and political legitimacy and their significance for a strategy to achieve a "higher" vision or maximalist program. Chapter 5 analyzes Diasporan realities and the ability of the Diaspora to perform the role it is assigned by maximalists. The last chapter argues against maximalism and in favor of normalcy.

At the end one may think that one answer is as legitimate as the other. But it is essential to understand what each preference entails as responsibility, risk, commitment, and possible consequence.

1.

Political Landscape I:
From Karabagh to Independence

How can one make sense of what is going on in Armenia? And in Karabagh? How can one assess competing claims by leaders and parties about what is good for Armenia and Karabagh? Is there a logic to the situation? Is there a way of assessing what is important and what is secondary among all the things one reads in newspapers and on the Internet, and one hears from visitors who have "the inside story"?

Part of the problem lies in the sources of information. With a few exceptions, the Armenian press in Armenia and in the Diaspora is either politically biased or lacks the resources and interest to do a professional job, or both. Most Armenian newspapers have to adopt a policy of checking and double-checking what they are reporting and to separate fact from rumor, information from opinion, and opinion from analysis.

In the case of Western sources, the problem is somewhat different. Western, particularly American, news outlets prefer the sensational, the conflictual, and the violent; to see their story printed, reporters often oblige. When reporting on countries that are of little significance to them, these reporters tend to follow the official line of their governments or holding companies.

Here, too, there are exceptions, but for the most part Western reporters suffer from the professional handicap of becoming "instant experts." They descend on a country, make not only political but also historical and moral judgments on anything and everything from the Constitution of the country, which most did not have time to read, to election laws, which they have not bothered to study. One reporter who covers Turkey for a major newspaper, having written at length on Turkish history in a number of columns, advised Armenians to forget the past. Reporters like to repeat themselves and other reporters. During the ten years of the Karabagh conflict, the parties to the conflict have managed wisely to leave out religion. Yet most news stories will introduce it as a conflict between "mostly Christian Armenia and largely Muslim Azerbaijan."

There is also the problem how readers outside of Armenia receive and digest the news. When the main context for reading the news is a need to confirm one's biases, when identities are invested in the news item, the readers are less likely to use critical judgment on the source, importance, and motivation of the news story.

A PEACEFUL BUT INCOMPLETE REVOLUTION

Nonetheless, it is possible to see some general trends in how political culture and history have evolved in Armenia.

The transition from a Soviet to an independent republic was peaceful and orderly. This remains an important and relevant fact, and credit must go to the Karabagh Committee and to the leaders of Armenia's Communist Party at the time. The country avoided internal clashes or worse. Despite a few attempts to bring violent change, stability prevailed. For that, credit must go first to the people of Armenia, and also to the Armenian National Movement (ANM), the successor organization to the Karabagh Committee, and to Armenia's first President.

There were also no witch hunts, no zeal to avenge the abuses of the past or to punish former leaders for the state of affairs at the time the ANM took over the government from the Communists in 1990. On the contrary, former leaders willing to contribute to the new state were given positions in the new administration and in industry and academia.

But there was also no critique of the former regime, no evaluation of the impact of Soviet rule on the economy, political culture, morals, and intellectual health of society. The "intellectual" class failed to examine the values by which intellectuals, writers, and artists were promoted and the impact of the values they represented on the spiritual and cultural well-being of society. Industry managers did not address the financial bankruptcy, management failure, infrastructural decay, and obsolete machinery that would make economic recovery difficult. Physicians failed to expose the antiquated and disastrous health system and medical practices, from Stalin's rules on childbirth to the treatment of the mentally ill. Educators failed to challenge an educational system that was antiquated and colonial in mentality, Stalinian in pedagogy, and rotten to the core.

Instead, once-privileged elites now tried to protect their positions by covering up the failures of the past, including their own. They opposed every effort to change and chimed in on the rhetoric of "intellectuals," who denounced the new administration and its problems, as if this were a new country and everything had started from scratch in 1990. They wanted everyone else to believe that independence and the new administration were responsible for everything from blockades to the barter economy, from poverty to prostitution, from corruption to crime. While under the Kocharian administration there were calls to prosecute those who were members of the administration between 1990 and 1997, there have been no similar calls for those who administered the country from 1921 to 1990 and who brought it to political, economic, and moral bankruptcy.

To become a normal, healthy society, Armenia needed radical change not only in the political and economic systems but also in the educational, judicial, health care, and social security systems. Resistance to change on the part of institutions, bureaucracies, professional groups, and privileged elites has been part of the cause for Armenia's inability to create a new and dignified society. To secure constituencies, political parties transformed resistance to change into respectable political agendas; "national ideology" provided a convenient cover for regressive politics.

POLITICS AND PARTIES

The citizens of Armenia have a basic, almost instinctive, distrust of political parties, all parties. The great majority of citizens are not members of or do not associate with any of them. This distrust began with their Communist Party experience during the Soviet period. The new parties did not give Armenians much reason to change their opinion, partly because of unrealistic expectations and partly as a result of the citizens' distaste for the behavior of the new parties and their leaders.

Armenians also have an ambivalent attitude toward the press and other news sources. Orally transmitted information—the rumor mill—which is certainly less reliable than the press, has more credibility with the average citizen. Yet Armenians remain avid readers of and listeners to news and commentaries. They are cynical, but they want to believe. They enjoy complaining, but their complaint does not necessarily constitute the basis of their vote.

Preferences for candidates reflect the sense of the candidates' demeanor as well as discourse and cannot necessarily be interpreted as support for the candidate's party. As one observer noted, Armenians are also immune to propaganda. The Soviet abuse of language has led them to mistrust leaders who talk too much, claim too much, and promise too much.

Political parties are still considered essential to democracies. But even in advanced democracies, maybe especially in advanced democracies, political parties no longer have the same power they used to enjoy in the nineteenth century or earlier in the twentieth century. Particularly in free market economies, much is decided outside the party structures and campaigns: Central banks, megabusiness, multinational corporations, and citizens' initiatives decide issues through processes that are outside party politics. And with changes in world economic structures and relations the traditional distinctions between the left and the right have become more blurred.

Political parties in Armenia display even less of an ability to reflect the concerns of voters in a manner credible to those voters. Nevertheless, even in Armenia, where their credibility in articulating problems and solutions is in question, parties still occupy the political landscape and remain the vehicles through which candidates and options are offered to the citizens.

Political parties in Armenia have been undergoing a process of mutation. Splits have appeared among those who had fought battles together. A number of parties currently functioning in Armenia are offshoots of the ANM, which was the governing party until February 1998: The National Democratic Union (NDU), led by Vazgen Manukian and Davit Vardanian, both members of the Karabagh Committee; the Civic Union of Scientists and Industrialists (CUSCI), led by Ashot Manucharian and Rafael Ghazarian, two other members of the Karabagh Committee; the Yerkrapahs, the group in Parliament responsible for Ter-Petrossian's loss of parliamentary support, was formed by Vazgen Sargsian, Defense Minister and a second generation ANM leader; and Shamiram, the women's organization founded by Vano Siradeghian, a member of the Karabagh Committee and leader of the ANM.

Two parties, the Communist Party of Armenia (CPA) led by Sergey Badalian and the Democratic Party of Armenia (DPA) led by Aram Sargsian were founded on the basis of the Armenian Communist Party of the Soviet period, which dissolved itself in 1991.

Three parties, the Armenian Revolutionary Federation or Dashnaktsutiune (ARF), the Armenian Democratic Liberal party or Ramkavar Party (ADL), and the Social Democratic Hunchakian Party (SDHP) were imported from the Diaspora following the adoption of the multiparty system in 1991.

Over the past decade some problems (including independence and institutions of sovereign statehood) have been resolved, making parties founded by Soviet era dissidents less relevant, even if their leaders are still active politically and command a following.

Most of the 74 political parties registered in Armenia by the end of 1998 have not been and may never be heard from. They are too small and too insignificant. They do not have field organizations, significant numbers of members, or well-known political figures at their head. Many other parties that are relatively well known are also small but enjoy notoriety due to the prominent personalities leading them.

Most of the parties that in 1998 claimed a following over 1 percent of the electorate were registered by 1992. Only two are newcomers. The Yerkrapahs started as an organization of war veterans and enjoyed the support of Defense Minister Vazgen Sargsian. At his urging, in the 1995 parliamentary elections President Ter-Petrossian and the ANM supported eight candidates from this group to be elected to the National Assembly. The Yerkrapah faction in Parliament, usually supportive of Ter-Petrossian, became the core group to oppose Ter-Petrossian in 1997 in his Karabagh policy. The Yerkrapahs absorbed the small Republican Party in 1998 and became a full-fledged political party in early 1999. The People's Party of Armenia was founded in mid-1998 by Karen Demirjian, following his strong showing in the 1998 presidential elections.

New parties are born and others disappear. Mutations and changes in party fortunes are quite normal and should not be considered, in and by themselves, a problem; the dominant role of personalities as opposed to programs could be a problem, however. That is the reason few parties can claim significant increases in their membership during the period that follows their initial appearance.

More important, a number of parties receive financial support from sources outside the country. External financing is illegal in Armenia, as in other countries. Whether for specific activities or as general support, external financing distorts public perception of the relative strength of parties and gives unfair advantage to some parties over others.

ISSUES AND AGENDAS

Analyzing parties through issues brings one closer to an understanding of Armenian politics. In addition to the problem of Karabagh, which was still largely in its premilitary phase, three major issues confronted the victorious, ANM-led non-Communist opposition in 1990: Would Armenia be an independent state or remain part of the USSR? Would Armenia opt for a multiparty democracy or remain a single-party regime? Should Armenia keep the centrally planned, socialist economic model or should it adopt a free market economy?

No one knew in 1988 where the Karabagh problem was headed. However, by 1991 everybody assumed independence for

Armenia would be declared that year, but international recognition of that independence was not expected for three or perhaps five years. While there was general consensus that a multiparty system and a free market economy would be adopted, it was not clear to what degree and how expeditiously each could be implemented without Moscow's recognition of Armenia's independence. Nonetheless, the fundamental choices were made by July 1991.

The collapse of the USSR in December 1991 expedited the recognition of Armenia's independence as well as the independence of all other Soviet republics, including those that had not asked or campaigned for it.

Old, often mute differences among movement leaders came to the surface, and new ones surfaced as the Armenian nation now faced a new set of issues.

The Environment

Some people might have forgotten that the mass movement of February 1988 was preceded by smaller street demonstrations in Yerevan in the fall of 1987 protesting the pollution generated by factories in and around Yerevan. The largest was a demonstration of about 5,000 people, unimpressive by subsequent standards but quite significant at the time.

The organizers were the loosely organized "Greens" of Armenia. The demonstrations raised the consciousness and curiosity of the population but did not produce any results. Beyond the importance of the issue in and of itself, the fact that a mass demonstration could take place is what registered in the minds of the citizens. First, it set a precedent for subsequent events: Demonstrations were now a possible method of raising an issue; there was a way outside the structure of government and party to articulate issues important to people.

Second, the environmental issue was absorbed by the Karabagh Movement. It was to be only one of many issues that brought people and all their grievances to the streets in February 1988. This is how the massive demonstrations moved very quickly from demands for Karabagh's unification with Armenia in February 1988 to an all-encompassing agenda of national rebirth by May 1988.

While still relevant, the environmental issue receded with the collapse of the economy. The first parliament of independent Armenia (1990–1995) did have a Green member who was not reelected to the National Assembly.

Nagorno Karabagh and the Karabagh Movement

The Karabagh conflict, which sparked the fire of the popular movement and came to symbolize the aspirations of the nation, evolved over a decade in more than one way. It was a political conflict turned violent. An administrative issue within one state, the USSR, was transformed into war between two independent states, with serious implications for regional and international security. Simultaneously, the significance of the conflict in domestic politics changed, as did its role in the national discourse, national economy, and in the programs of parties.

A distinction should be made between the problem of Nagorno Karabagh and the Karabagh Movement in Armenia.

In Karabagh, the Karabagh Movement was and remained a single-issue movement: the future of Karabagh.

In Armenia, the Karabagh issue sparked the movement but could not limit its agenda and evolution. If speeches made during February and March 1988 were limited to Karabagh, by May 1988 the leaders of the movement were addressing issues of democracy, value systems, corruption, the nonnational character of the state (Russification and the birthrate of the ethnic Azeri population) and, eventually, independence.

This evolution of the Karabagh issue was due to three factors.

First, when the regional government of Stepanakert, capital of the then autonomous region of Nagorno Karabagh, raised the issue of unification with Armenia on 20 February 1988, the expectations, both in Karabagh and in Armenia, were that it would be resolved quickly in favor of Karabagh's request. Adjustments to the internal administrative boundaries within the USSR had occurred over a dozen times in the history of the USSR. Furthermore, individual activists who had had conversations in Moscow had concluded that "Moscow" would respond favorably to a popular request for such a readjustment. It was, after all, the period of glasnost and perestroika and de-Stalinization. If corrections were being made in the political and economic system imposed by Stalinism, there was reason to believe that the third pillar of the Soviet order, the internal boundary system unfair to many ethnic groups, could also be changed.

Moscow's failure to respond positively and anti-Armenian pogroms in Sumgait in late February and early March 1988 led Armenians to question the system itself: After all, being part of the Soviet Union was supposed to have guaranteed the security of Armenians.

The change was not too different from the evolution of Armenian political thinking in late nineteenth and early twentieth centuries. Peaceful petitions by moderate Armenians for reforms in the Ottoman Empire, ostensibly supported by the Great Powers, produced no results. Moderates gave way to revolutionaries; the state responded with massacres. Revolutionaries then started asking why Western countries were not systematic in their support for reforms. The answer was simple: The imperialistic interests of capitalist Europeans and the nondemocratic character of Russia. This answer led some of the revolutionaries to seek the solution of the "Armenian Question" in the radical overhaul of the world system. Some joined the anti-imperialistic and revolutionary European and Russian movement and adopted Marxist and marxistic, not just socialistic, political ideologies.

A second important reason the Karabagh demonstrations evolved into a movement of national renaissance was the significance of street demonstrations for the common citizen. As important as the issue of Karabagh was (or became) for most people, what mattered was the symbolism of effectively articulating opposition to the state for the first time. The system was politically and morally bankrupt; people were dissatisfied; and now they had a chance to join with the rest of the nation to make a personal statement about that system. Their disgust was not related solely to the status of Karabagh. Rather, it was related to the system that ruled every aspect of their lives. Karabagh became the trigger and the symbol of the protest movement against the system, but it did not limit the movement's agenda. This also explains the change of leadership of the movement from the single-issue nationalist Communists, such as Zori Balayan, Sylva Kaputikian, and Igor Muratian, to the newer, largely unknown faces of Vazgen Manukian, Levon Ter-Petrossian, Babken Ararktsian, and the others.

The third factor was the difference between the legal status of Karabagh and Armenia. Karabagh was an autonomous region within Azerbaijan, with limited access to and interaction with Soviet-wide institutions and no international standing, while Armenia was a constituent republic of the USSR. As the struggle took shape, Armenia's interaction with Moscow, Azerbaijan, and the rest of the world compelled it to define issues in the context of all other dimensions of its relations with Soviet authorities and the international community.

As the Karabagh Committee relentlessly pursued the goal of obtaining a change in administrative boundaries that would reunite Karabagh with Armenia, Armenia's only legal and ruling party, Armenian SSR Communist Party, responded with a timid attempt to control the movement. While some officials sympathized with the movement's primary goal, most were concerned with its direction and implications. When the mass movement became compelling and the slogans began to transcend the boundaries of the original issue, the Communist Party and government bodies began to co-opt the movement in a futile attempt to prevent its radicalization. Radicalization would challenge Communist rule and the status of Armenia within the USSR, and the issues of democracy and independence would rise to the surface.

The imprisonment of the movement leaders by Soviet Armenian authorities following the December 1988 earthquake turned out to be a major mistake. Yet allowing these leaders to organize popular support for the relief efforts would also have been a mistake: The movement would have de facto replaced a government that could no longer inspire or organize. By the time popular frustration with a bureaucratic and corrupt government compelled Moscow to release the prisoners in June 1989, the landscape had changed substantially, and the Karabagh Committee began to think about making a move for power. In 1989 the movement became an organization, ANM, with a wide-ranging political agenda: It demanded nothing less than the revamping of Armenian political and economic structures, plus the resolution of the problem of Karabagh by uniting it with Armenia. The ANM offered a program of national rebirth.

Despite their differences, the ANM and government had a civil relationship for the most part. The elections to the Supreme Soviet of Armenia in the spring of 1990 brought the ANM-led coalition into power. The Communists fought hard but lost the presidency of that body. The Supreme Soviet became a vehicle of change, a true legislative body, with direct control over the Council of Ministers and executive powers. That was the beginning of institutional and political transformation.

With the assumption of power by the ANM and recognition of Armenia's independence by the international community, the character of the Karabagh problem changed drastically. Karabagh became, by definition, one item on the agenda of the new government and new sovereign state. While Karabagh too declared its independence unilaterally in 1992, Ter-Petrossian refrained from recognizing that declaration. Nonetheless, the relationship between Armenia and Karabagh remained cordial and sound.

In June 1992 efforts at mediation between Azerbaijan and the Armenian side by Russia and Iran were replaced by negotiations mediated by the Organization for Security and Cooperation in Europe (OSCE, CSCE at the time). Both Armenia and Azerbaijan had joined the organization as independent states soon after the recognition of their independence. Although the original mandate of the OSCE was to find a solution to the problem of the status of Karabagh at an international conference to be held in Minsk, Belarus, intensification of the military confrontation on the ground compelled the mediators to seek a halt to the fighting as the dominant item on the agenda of what came to be known as the Minsk Group within the OSCE.

Participation in these negotiations became the next contentious issue. Karabagh, invited as "an interested party," first refused to participate. Karabagh was supported by opposition parties in Armenia which, in the summer of 1992 organized street demonstrations demanding that Armenia recognize Karabagh's independence. The parties pressing the issue included the two communist parties, Vazgen Manukian's NDU, Paruyr Hayrikian's National Self-Determination Union (NSDU), and the ARF, which, having failed to achieve electoral success in Armenia, had sought to strengthen its position in Karabagh.

Ter-Petrossian refused. He argued that a permanent and durable solution would require reaching a solution through negotiations based necessarily on compromises on both sides, that Armenia's recognition of Karabagh's independence would foreclose all negotiations and the problem would remain unresolved.

Karabagh eventually agreed to participate in the OSCE-led negotiations. The Minsk Group negotiations never moved on to the status problem but led to a series of proposals, none of which were accepted by all three parties to the conflict. At the same time, a proposal presented in September 1997 was accepted by Azerbaijan and Armenia as a basis of renewed negotiations, but was rejected by Karabagh. It was also rejected by some of Ter-Petrossian's associates in his administration, leading to the resignation of Ter-Petrossian and the election of Robert Kocharian as President of Armenia.

Political parties or political leaders have rarely presented clearly articulated views on the solution of the Karabagh problem or a strategy on how to achieve it, before or after Ter-Petrossian's resignation. Many opposition parties, such as the communist groups and the ARF, reacted strongly against any mention of compromise, but offered no constructive plan for the solution of the conflict. Others spoke of compromise but did not clarify what they were ready to compromise. Nor Ughi (New Path), an offshoot of the ANM led by Ktrich Sardarian and Ashot Bleyan, offered the simplest, though the least popular, solution: to secure guarantees for the rights of Karabagh Armenians and leave Karabagh within Azerbaijan. Nor Ughi leaders argued that Karabagh would be the albatross that would choke Armenia, cause the loss of its ability to function independently, and the mechanism by which traditional thinking would reenter Armenian foreign policy.

This issue is further explored in the next two chapters. But any attempt to identify differences in approaches to the solution to the Karabagh problem raises a number of difficulties. First, the word *compromise* was politicized before it was clarified. Second, the issue became easily manipulated for political purposes and parties have been sending conflicting signals. In 1998 President Kocharian's advisers included Vahan Hovannisian, leader of the ARF of Armenia; Paruyr Hayrikian, of the NSDU; and Aram Sargsian, leader of the ADP. Davit Vardanian, Vazgen Manukian's deputy in the NDU, is director of the Supervisory Agency in the President's office. All represent parties that demanded that Ter-Petrossian recognize Karabagh's unilateral declaration of independence in 1992. None has raised that possibility since joining Kocharian in the President's office, nor have they demanded, at least publicly, that Karabagh be annexed to Armenia.

Independence

Beyond the problem of Karabagh, the political agenda facing Armenia in 1990 consisted of items that would shape the country's character: Should Armenia remain part of the USSR or become an independent country? Should Armenia have a single-party or multiparty system? Should Armenia have a centrally planned economy based largely on state-owned means of production or should it adopt a free market economy?

The first major issue to confront the parties was independence.

Even though some members might have had independence in mind all along, the Karabagh Committee had not started with such a goal in mind. The goal of independence followed the logic of the internal situation, some said the logic of history—Armenian and world history—and at the end independence was inevitable.

Hambartsum Galstian, the youngest member of the committee and the future Mayor of Yerevan, was one who believed that the whole story would end up with independence. He was the first committee member I came to know somewhat closely during a trip to Yerevan in May 1988. A young ethnologist active in the Communist Youth organization, he tried to convince me, a Diasporan historian and still an ARF member, that independence was where Armenia was heading, which was a good thing, just as an ARF member should have or was supposed to have thought. But this ARF'er was skeptical.

Eventually, events left no alternative. Once it made the choice, the ANM went all the way for Armenian independence, but did so peacefully and according to the USSR Law on Secession enacted by Gorbachev.

The last chance to stop the march toward independence was the election of the President of the Presidium of the Supreme Soviet of the Armenian SSR following the spring 1990 general elections to that Soviet-style legislature. There were, in essence, two parties represented at the time in the Supreme Soviet: the official Communist Party (CP) and the ANM-led coalition, the opposition. This was not an easy election. The result of the election of the Supreme Soviet president would indicate the direction in which the country was headed on major issues. Neither side was assured of a clear majority. Most Communists voted for Vladimir Movsisian, the First Secretary and that party's candidate. At the end, most newcomers and a few Communists, including the pivotal decision of Vigen Khachatrian, Secretary of the CP Gugark Regional organization, voted for Levon Ter-Petrossian, the ANM candidate. Movsisian lost but did not hold a grudge against Ter-Petrossian, nor did Ter-Petrossian against Movsisian. Movsisian subsequently served as Head of the State Agency for Refugees, Minister of Agriculture, and provincial Governor under Ter-Petrossian. Other Communists also joined the new administration. Gagik Harutiunian, Head of the CP Central Committee's Economic Affairs Department, for example, was elected a Vice-Chairman of the Supreme Soviet, then Vice-President of the Republic (1991–1995) on the Ter-Petrossian ticket, and he was appointed President of the Constitutional Court following the creation of that body in 1995.

As the 21 September referendum drew closer, the CP knew it was too weak to resist the inexorable march toward a declaration of independence. It knew Armenian independence would mean loss of power. Some party members had genuine concerns about the ability of Armenia to stand on its own feet. They were also concerned about what Moscow would say about Armenia and its loyalty. Nonetheless, they knew they could not do much to slow that march. For the most part, the last leaders of Soviet Armenia acted honorably and in a manner that saved the nation and the republic any new trauma. The ARF, too, however reluctantly, found it impossible to oppose independence, although it had been the founder of the first republic in 1918 and bearer of the torch of independence since 1919. The other two Diasporan parties supported independence, although historically they were the ones with reservations on that subject.

None of the parties that were founded following the adoption by the Supreme Soviet of the multiparty system in Armenia opposed independence. Most supported it enthusiastically. Since 1997, however, the new Communist Party of Armenia (CPA) has started agitating for Armenia's integration in the Russia-Belarus Union.

Economic Reforms

The question of Armenia's future economic system appeared on the national agenda even before independence. Most people shared the sense that, whatever the original intent and promise of the Soviet model, something had gone terribly wrong. Few were ready to defend it. Adopting the free market system was as much a political statement as a choice of economic system. The attraction was toward the liberal world, politically and economically. The two went together. It was natural, therefore, that the Armenian SSR Supreme Soviet under ANM leadership voted overwhelmingly in favor of a free market economy. Neither the ANM nor its offshoots that ended up in opposition have significantly strayed from that path.

Since independence, economic reform has been a problem more challenging than the Karabagh conflict, more difficult than developing institutions of statehood, more defying than winning a war, more challenging than writing a working Constitution, more intricate than creating a civil society, and more misunderstood than the pervasive corruption. Yet this problem of economic reform is related to and possibly underpins all other problems. For the citizen, this problem translates into the right to work, the right to make a decent living, in dignity, by one's labor and includes other rights that ensue from it.

The problem begins with the term *reform* itself. Calling what needed to be done *reform* of the economy was to misdiagnose the problem and, eventually, delay the real cure. Even the word *transformation* does not come close to recognizing the depth of what needed to be done.

Economic reform signaled a change of the system from centralized planning to a market economy. The state had to relinquish control of an economy dictated by a political ideology. That much was clear. But the center of planning had not been Yerevan; it had been Moscow. What passed for an economy in Armenia had little economic logic and did not make sense outside the parameters of the Soviet bloc. It was one thing to change the centrally planned economy of an independent state, where the problem was the ownership of the means of production, so to speak. It was another thing to begin with the leftovers of an economy that had produced the tires of a car in Yerevan, the body in Estonia, and the engine in Kazakhstan—all to be finally assembled as a car in Ukraine! The logic of the economy was not only ideological but also imperial.

The industrial base of the economy faced other problems as well. Most machinery in factories was painfully outdated, and the quality of goods produced could rarely compete in the world market. For two decades, when the world economy had been revolutionized, the Soviet planners had made no serious investments in the infrastructure of the country, in roads or communications. Moreover, few, if any, in the country had any concept of marketing, and still fewer knew the actual markets in which the products were sold or bartered by the central planners. The country needed a new economy and not just the reform of the old one. It would have been easier to begin from scratch than to build on what Armenia started out with.

A market economy required much that was lacking: a new commercial code and lawyers and judges who understood it; an independent judiciary; customs and tax codes and services. A market economy required a legal infrastructure and the institutions to go with it. Most of all, it required capital investments. Changing the laws on ownership was hardly sufficient to change the system.

Moreover, neither the country nor the citizenry had the capital to invest in change. The uncertainties compelled the holders of what capital there was to invest in short-term trade rather than in long-term industrial production that had little chance to find its way to world markets. Armenia itself was also too small and too poor to constitute a viable market for foreign investments that could replace or complement domestic capital.

Further, two more related factors came into play: the blockades, which made the import of raw materials and the export of finished products extremely expensive if not impossible, and the war, which claimed priority on existing yet rare resources. The Karabagh conflict had also made impossible the creation of a larger, regional market for goods that could be produced in Armenia.

Each of these factors would have presented a challenge to any government. Their confluence tested the intellect, imagination, patience, and endurance of any official who tried to deal with them. Whatever the degree of progress made in this direction, there is no doubt that at the end, the economic dimension is the one affecting immediately and on a daily basis almost every aspect of the lives of Armenians—as individuals, as families, as a society. Independence and democracy, national visions and international aspirations, spiritual yearnings and cultural achievements, traditional ties and moral choices flounder when up against the rock of one reality: the poverty in which the majority of citizens had sunk with the collapse of a bankrupt economy. As elsewhere, for the citizen to link independence and poverty and to ask "What, after all, is the advantage of independent statehood?" could be a temptation difficult to resist.

The problem with the transformation of the economic system was that not many people knew much about a market economy.

What they knew were bits and pieces of models of other countries. Even fewer—in Armenia, in the former USSR republics, or in the rest of the world—knew how to transform the system. There was no first-hand knowledge or accumulated experience of mechanisms for the transformation of a centrally planned economy to a free market one in a republic in which the economy was anything but national.

In 1991 Armenia denationalized the agricultural sector, the first of the former USSR republics to do so, distributing 90 percent of arable land free to the peasants who were working on it. As radical and welcome as the policy was, the agrarian revolution remained incomplete without adequate provisions for the use of machinery, credits, storage, and transportation to markets.

Large-scale privatization of shops, medium-size enterprises, and major industrial plants followed slowly. Each phase and method was accompanied by complaints and charges—sometimes legitimate and often absurd—in which systemic failures played as much a role as favoritism, nepotism, and corruption.

Not until the end of 1993, after two years of experimentation and groping, with the involvement of the International Monetary Fund and the World Bank, were the enthusiastic yet haphazard reforms organized around macro-economics goals and strategies.

The full meaning of a market economy and its implications emerged over time. So did the significance of the blockades and of the Russian decision to leave Armenia and other former Soviet republics out of the ruble zone, thus compelling Armenia to introduce a national currency earlier than planned, and the war, which constantly challenged projections.

Over the past eight years debate on economic issues has focused on mistakes in the planning and execution of the dismantling of a centrally planned economy, rather than on whether to dismantle it or not; divergences covered the manner in which the new system was being erected, not whether or not to erect a new system.

During his 1996 presidential campaign, Vazgen Manukian focused on this aspect and linked three arguments: The administration was mishandling economic reforms; the administration was unable to bring in foreign investments; and government officials were corrupt, clannish, and Mafia bosses. The result was the poverty to which the former middle class, most of the citizenry, had sunk.

Regarding the first argument, Manukian and his NDU, as well as the other parties that eventually supported his candidacy in 1996, explained that government officials were incompetent and uninterested in the welfare of the people, indifferent to the future of the country, and absorbed in securing personal gain; they argued that the NDU and other opposition parties had a higher degree of dedication and would be more efficient in implementing economic reforms and attracting foreign investments.

The opposition discussed corruption in moral terms. They exploited a popular definition of the word *Mafia*, applied to anyone who made money quickly, whether legally or illegally. They also lumped together corruption on high levels of government and the petty corruption of traffic policemen and bureaucrats.

The solution was to bring the opposition to power. The new administration would be efficient, clean, and dedicated to national ideals and values. The opposition would make Armenia a great nation. Science and industry would restored, along with morality. As a practical step, Manukian promised to increase salaries of the state sector employees tenfold. These employees were still the majority of wage earners.

The counter-argument, not always so clearly articulated, was that there was no magic solution to the problem of poverty, no quick fixes to the economic crisis. Significant changes required steady legal and institutional reforms as well as improvement in the security environment in the region to ensure foreign investments. It was not possible to provide substantial increases in the salaries of civil servants without an increase in productivity and real growth in the economy. The only other way to increase salaries was the printing of money, which would increase inflation and erode the buying power of the citizen as well as his trust in the currency.

Furthermore, "making the factories work" was a good electoral promise, but it was not made clear how this would be done, with what capital and machinery, to produce what goods, and how to transport and which markets to sell at.

Corruption, a problem more rampant under the Soviets but also illegal to reveal and discuss at the time, was in essence an economic and not a moral problem. Legal measures and disciplinary actions would fail at the end to uproot corruption as long as the judge, prosecutor, bureaucrat, and policeman did not earn enough to make a decent living. For that part of the electorate that had turned skepticism into an artform, if not an analytical system, it was better to keep "those who had already filled their pockets" in power, rather than to bring a new cast of players who would have to start all over.

The CPA, under Badalian, had not joined the group of opposition parties supporting Manukian's candidacy. Still, the guardians of the old faith also had reservations in the area of economic policies, but they did not express them forcefully in the early stages. Their confidence had been shaken, and they lacked credibility. Even if they had a good argument in favor of a moderate or gradual change that took into consideration the social impact of these radical changes, the Communists would not have been taken seriously.

Gradually, however, as the economy hit bottom and the middle class disappeared in Armenia, the communist parties became bolder and criticized the government not just on methods but also on substance. But they were not able to articulate an alternative that made sense to the voter.

A more radical critique of the economic reforms, at least on the conceptual level, was introduced in 1996 by the CUSCI, which selected Ashot Manucharian, the former Senior Adviser to Ter-Petrossian, as its presidential candidate. The CUSCI also maintained its independent candidacy in 1996. An ingenious though not always a productive thinker, Manucharian recognized that the Soviet model had not worked, but neither would the capitalist model, he argued. Manucharian displayed a genuine Marxian, even if not Marxist, concern for the working and unemployed classes. He proposed a "third way." Unfortunately, he failed to provide any details. He did insist, nonetheless, that this third way was not relevant just to Armenia; it had universal significance, and not only in the realm of economic choices but also in terms of human and civilizational values. The voters failed to appreciate him; in the 1996 presidential elections he received less than 1 percent of the vote.

Similarly, major candidates in the 1998 presidential elections failed to present a challenge to the system that had been evolving. Both major candidates, Robert Kocharian and Karen Demirjian, did speak of the "social" dimension in economic policy. The difference between the two major candidates consisted of the more cautious attitude that Demirjian displayed toward the privatization of major factories compared to Kocharian.

Only the communist parties have offered to reverse course. And the combined percentage these parties have garnered since 1991 has not exceeded 7 percent. Kocharian's aggressive policy of privatizing major factories and industries, such as the cognac factory and communications, has produced resistance among some of the opposition parties that are, nevertheless, for the most part, supporters of a market economy.

Political Reforms

When the ANM-led coalition won control of the Supreme Soviet in the summer of 1990, there was general agreement that Armenia should become a multiparty, liberal democracy. New parties were established, and some members of the Supreme Soviet joined parties that had not existed in Armenia before. By mid-1991, the Law on Political and Public Organizations, the Law on the Freedom of the Press, the Law on Freedom of Religion and Conscience (which also separated church and state while recognizing the special position of the Apostolic Church in Armenian history and culture), were ratified by the parliament.

While it was generally agreed that Armenia needed a Constitution, there were two views on how to proceed. Ter-Petrossian and the ANM believed that if the Constitution was to have any degree of respectability, it would have to reflect the country's needs and endure the test of time. Such a document could not be drafted without some testing and deliberation. Paruyr Hayrikian of the NSDU insisted that a Constitution should be adopted immediately. The ANM prevailed.

A Constitutional Commission was formed in 1992. It included scholars and judges as well leaders of parties represented in parliament. As opposition parties hardened their position against the administration, over the next three years some parties ended their participation in the process. The Commission completed its draft in 1995, and the Constitution was adopted by a general referendum in July 1995.

The Constitution was not successful in resolving some questions on the kind of democracy Armenia should have. In the early days of the ANM-led administration, the Supreme Soviet had full legislative and a degree of executive authority. The Supreme Soviet's Presidium, consisting of the chairmen of the permanent committees and the president, vice-president, and secretary of that body, enjoyed some executive power, sharing it with the Council of Ministers. The first Prime Minister, Vazgen Manukian, who was still in the ANM, did not feel he had enough independence and power to effectively run the executive branch. After a few months in office, in the fall of 1990 he asked the Supreme Soviet for special powers for six months in order to effectively implement the changes in the government and to run the economy. These powers were given to him.

When the six months expired, he returned to Parliament in the spring of 1991 with a request to extend and expand those special powers. Parliament refused, saying that such broad powers were equivalent to a dictatorship. Manukian then argued that what the country needed were a clear separation of the two branches of government and a strong executive president, elected directly by the people, with a clear mandate to lead the country. The Supreme Soviet agreed and passed the Law on the Presidency in July 1991. Manukian had thought he would be the natural choice. But in the face of Ter-Petrossian's overwhelming popularity, he withdrew his candidacy and started organizing his own party, the NDU.

Ter-Petrossian's election in September 1991 marked only the beginning of the battle on the powers of the presidency. A number of unsuccessful candidates, who had earlier advocated a strong presidency and had voted for the law defining the future president's powers, began arguing that what the country needed was a parliamentary democracy. Paruyr Hayrikian, one of the most ardent advocates of a strong presidency, became one of its most insistent critics.

A serious study and comparative analysis of the 1991 Law on the Presidency and the 1995 Constitution (something most foreign journalists commenting in a cavalier fashion on the subject and opposition parties have not bothered to do) will find that Armenia's constitutional system is a mixture of the presidential and the parliamentary systems.

The President of Armenia is powerful if he or she has the support of the majority in parliament. If the opposition controls Parliament, the President is reduced largely to a figurehead. A parliamentary majority in opposition means a Prime Minister from the opposition. A Prime Minister from the opposition means control over most appointments since the President can choose only from nominees offered by the Prime Minister. In this important respect, Armenia's system is similar to the French Constitution, which has already had two instances of "co-habitation."

The Law on the Presidency adopted in 1991 provided that an override of a presidential veto required a two thirds vote of the legislature. The 1995 Constitution changed that to a simple majority; that is, a President could suggest changes to the National Assembly in a law that it had already passed; the President could object, argue, and cajole. But only a simple majority is still needed for an override of the veto, and the National Assembly need not consider the President's objections as anything more than suggestions. The National Assembly could pass the same law, and the President would have no choice but to sign it.

Between the process of appointments and vetoing, there is not much the President can do if the opposition controls Parliament. In fact, technically speaking and from the constitutional point of view, that is exactly what happened in February 1998. The Prime Minister and two ministers, all appointees of the President, refused to accept a foreign policy decision of the President. There was a stalemate within the executive, with authority remaining with the President. But the President's authority dissipated as soon as a group of supporters that had made up his majority in the

National Assembly changed their position and became part of the opposition. The moment the President lost the majority in the Parliament, he could no longer fight the battle on policy.

The battle over the powers of the presidency continued after Ter-Petrossian's resignation. Most candidates in the 1998 presidential elections (the ANM did not present a candidate), including Kocharian, still supported a change in the Constitution so as to take power from the presidency and give it to the Parliament; some called for an outright parliamentary system. Once elected, though, Kocharian realized that the President's powers were really not that great. No candidate in the field, once elected, would have reached a different conclusion.

The Constitution of Armenia certainly needs to be amended. It contains some internal contradictions, and parts of it are unclear. Yet it is a better Constitution than most people believe. Amendments should not be predicated on which leader occupies the office of the President or on what party controls Parliament.

The second major controversy regarding the progress of democratization in Armenia revolves around the legitimacy of the referendum on the Constitution and of parliamentary elections in 1995, and of the presidential elections in 1996 and 1998. That procedural irregularities and violations of the law, sometimes on the part of opposition groups as well as supporters of the governing camp, occurred in each of these occasions, has not been disputed. Whether these violations and other fraudulent actions would have changed the result of any or all of these votes cannot be ascertained without a systematic review in a less politically charged atmosphere.

But it is possible to offer some observations that are relevant regardless of the results of future inquiries in this area. Whatever the violations in electoral law, so far the problem has consisted of violations of the laws that protect the fairness and openness of elections. None of the administrations have so far suggested eliminating the laws or the adopted system.

Members of some opposition parties elected to the National Assembly in 1995 boycotted the sessions of that body. These parties also rejected the Constitution adopted the same year and refused to recognize the results of the 1996 presidential elections on the grounds that all three votes were fraudulent. Yet, once Ter-Petrossian had resigned, Vazgen Manukian's NDU, Paruyr Hayrikian's NSDU, the ARF, and Aram Sargsian's DPA all returned to the same National Assembly; their leaders have become advisors to President Kocharian, and all are working on the basis of the legitimacy granted to Kocharian by the same Constitution they had rejected.

Parties supportive of Kocharian's candidacy, who in 1996 had relied on foreign observers to prove that the presidential elections of that year were fraudulent, dismissed similar conclusions of the same foreign observers regarding the 1998 presidential elections as an attempt by foreign powers to weaken Armenia's position and as "anti-Armenian."

The democratization process was set back, according to some people, by two decisions Ter-Petrossian made during his tenure in office: The banning of the ARF and the use of the army to control the crowds on the evening of 26 September 1996 following the presidential elections.

In late December 1994 Ter-Petrossian signed an order banning the ARF on national security grounds, having received evidence that the party was responsible for criminal acts and was engaged in illegal activities. Within 48 hours of this order, the Attorney General asked the Supreme Court to decree the same on two grounds: terroristic activities and violation of the Law on Political and Public Organizations, which included the provision that no political organization can be governed by a leadership from abroad and by noncitizens. The Supreme Court rejected the first argument, stating that responsibility for crimes must be proven in court before punishment is meted. The Court upheld the President's ban on the second ground, instructing the party to provide evidence that it had complied with the law before the ban could be lifted.

The basic law governing political parties had been passed in 1991 with the support of the ARF members of the legislature. No state can permit noncitizens—of whatever ethnic origin—residing in foreign countries to constitute the leadership of a political party functioning in that state. If other countries do not have such a ban articulated clearly as law, it is because they do not face the same problem, not because such provisions are alien to functioning democracies. Also, the Constitution of a number of functioning democracies allows the banning of political parties (or of groups otherwise prone to violence but passing as political parties or religious groups) under specific circumstances.

The ADL registered in Armenia in 1991 as the ADL of Armenia, an entity organizationally separate from its Diasporan counterpart. The same year, the ARF insisted on registering the party in Armenia as an integral part of the worldwide organization. Although this was against the law, the Ministry of Justice registered the party in the spirit of inclusiveness, as a gesture toward the Diaspora. But it did so with the understanding that the ARF would, over time, adjust its structures to Armenian law. But the ARF did not comply with the law, despite warnings by the Ministry of Justice in 1993 and 1994 that its status was in question. What was tolerated before December 1994 was not deemed acceptable when that tolerance was abused.

In September 1996 the troops were ordered into the streets following the storming of the Parliament building, the kidnapping of the President of the National Assembly, and the beating of the two Vice-presidents of that body. The storming had been clearly engineered by the coalition around the Manukian candidacy, including the leaders of the NDU, ARF, and other individuals. Manukian and his associates had determined, long before the ballots were cast, that if he lost the elections, it could only be because the elections were rigged. He declared himself a winner even before the ballots were counted. Subsequently, he called on "the people" to take matters into their own hands, and some did.

It is important to note that in both cases is there not only an element of violence and destabilization, but also an a priori acceptance by the two political parties, the NDU and the ARF, of violence and "revolutionary" means to achieve power.

As early as 1991, Manukian had argued in a newspaper article that while Armenia should be a democracy, Armenia's democracy need not necessarily follow the Western model. Subsequently, and especially before and after the 1996 elections, Manukian often evoked the preamble of the U.S. Declaration of Independence, which, in his view, validated his inclination to use violence to overthrow a government he considered unacceptable.

In fact, if one read carefully the program of the opposition parties that joined efforts behind Manukian's candidacy in 1996, two points of their three-point program called for the suspension of the Constitution and the dissolution of the Parliament. A fourth point, apparently agreed upon on the eve of the release of the program and communicated by Hayrikian but not included in the printed text, was the formation of a security council to govern the country until such time as a new constitution would be drafted and adopted. In turn, ARF leaders in Armenia had on many occasions declared themselves above the law, in the name of "higher" or "national" ideals.

These incidents are symptomatic of much more than the usual struggle for power among personalities, elites, and parties. Much has changed since Ter-Petrossian's resignation, but the revolutionary zeal of some of the parties has not. Ter-Petrossian's removal would bring closer the moment when they could come to power. From that perspective, these parties see Kocharian as an intermediate figure who could never satisfy their needs and programs.

Ter-Petrossian's resignation raised more questions than the issue of succession. It revealed strains but also some strengths in the system. It also marked fundamental differences in the understanding of statehood and nationhood between those who want to shape the future of Armenia after Ter-Petrossian.

2.

A Resignation

The single most important event that must be analyzed in order to help us understand current battles and imagine future developments is the resignation in February 1998 of President Levon Ter-Petrossian.

This event is important in and by itself. It marks the demise of the first-ever directly elected executive head of state in Armenian history. He had dominated a decade full of upheavals and had tried to give Armenia a new and fresh outlook on the world.

That resignation in February 1998 tells much about the political culture of Armenia and the Armenian people; about the personalities involved—Ter-Petrossian and his antagonists—in Armenia and abroad; about the strengths and weaknesses of institutions and of the Constitution; and about the intricate relations between foreign interests and domestic political forces. The break in the continuum of history reveals underlying currents and future trends that might not otherwise reveal themselves in the day-to-day accounts.

THE CONVENTIONAL WISDOM

Why did Ter-Petrossian resign? What problem was his resignation supposed to resolve? Was the problem resolved, in fact, with his resignation?

It has been argued that Ter-Petrossian had lost the support of the people. This may be true, but the relevance of this loss to his resignation requires more analysis than has been offered. Presidents of the United States and prime ministers of other countries often lose popular support before the end of their term but continue to govern until new scheduled elections. Negative public opinion is not sufficient to change presidents or governments. When people vote, they vote for people to hold their elected positions for a determined period of time. No doubt, when a president loses public support, he has more difficulty governing; his resignation also emboldens his opponents. But, as is discussed below, the dissatisfaction with Ter-Petrossian and/or with his administration has little to do with his solution to the problem that was central to his resignation, Nagorno Karabagh. It is interesting to note that after ten years of leadership under the most trying circumstances and challenges, Ter-Petrossian still received the support of about half the voters against a united opposition and a formidable candidate.

Of course, there are also people who question the validity of Ter-Petrossian's second election in 1996 as well as of the Constitution that determines the President's mandate. Whether the irregularities in the voting changed the outcome of the elections will be determined when historians have a good look at all the evidence. Until then, most views are based on belief and politics.

However important for the development of democracy in Armenia and for history, the validity of his mandate is irrelevant for the purposes of this discussion: Ter-Petrossian resigned under pressure from associates who had accepted the results of the election and the legitimacy of the Constitution and who were serving under him on the basis of the results of that election and Constitution.

Ter-Petrossian resigned under pressure from powerful members of his own cabinet who opposed his acceptance of the OSCE Minsk Group Co-Chairmen's September 1997 draft proposal for the resolution of the Nagorno Karabagh conflict. His Prime Minister, Robert Kocharian, Defense Minister Vazgen Sargsian, and Interior and Security Minister Serge Sargsian argued that the proposal was not in the interests of Armenia and Karabagh. That was the headline. That was the conventional wisdom, not only in Armenia, but also in the Diaspora and in the international press. Of course, Karabagh was at the heart of the conflict within the administration, and differences existed between the President and three important members of the cabinet.

Yet, some questions need to be posed. A momentous event such as the resignation of the President takes place on 3 February 1998, following four months of public squabbling. The Prime Minister becomes acting President and is then elected President in special elections in March. Almost six months of political trauma, however, fail to reveal the choices on the resolution of the problem that compelled the President to resign. The public still does not know exactly what the differences between Ter-Petrossian and Kocharian were.

Public debate on how to solve the problem of Nagorno Kara-bagh—or how not to solve it—was the most serious casualty of events surrounding Ter-Petrossian's resignation. For those who were happy to see him leave office, debate did not matter; tidbits of characterizations and innuendoes were acceptable as basis for his resignation. Those who asked him to leave did not reveal what it was that Ter-Petrossian was ready to accept that would have constituted a giveaway or, in the view of some, treason. Ter-Petrossian himself has not explained it; neither have his supporters, on his request. Not to reveal the contents of documents and confidential negotiations until an agreement was initialed had been part of the ground rules agreed on with the international mediators.

The near silence of those who respected Ter-Petrossian's capabilities and policies, coupled with the vociferous gloating, often public and occasionally repulsive, of those who hated him, does not constitute debate. A new presidential election caused by Ter-Petrossian's resignation failed to elicit a discussion of alternative solutions to a conflict that has bedeviled Armenia since its rebirth as an independent state.

Informed debate requires information, naturally. Writers on the subject, Armenian and non-Armenian, did not have the necessary information on the OSCE proposal. But they also did not bother to admit to their ignorance, nor were they able to resist the temptation to pontificate. Only a few individuals recognized the problem inherent in having a credible position without credible information.

Ter-Petrossian's resignation involves much more than the fate of one person, or his place in history; it is more than the issue of the constitutionality of the process. His resignation touches on our perception of the state, of power, and of the kind of discourse we need to define problems and to make choices.

To appreciate the full complexity of the circumstances surrounding the resignation and its significance, a few observations are in order.

Ter-Petrossian did not resign under pressure from his traditional antagonists, the conventional opposition: The Communist Party of Armenia (CPA), the Democratic Party of Armenia (DPA), the National Democratic Union (NDU), the National Self-Determination Union (NSDU), and the Armenian Revolutionary Federation (ARF). Rather, the resignation was caused by the position taken by individuals with whom he had worked closely over the last decade, associates who had high respect for him, who would have preferred, by and large, that he continue in office and who did not believe he would resign when faced with opposition to his peace plan: Robert Kocharian, the former President of Nagorno Karabagh whom Ter-Petrossian had invited to serve as Prime Minister of Armenia; Vazgen Sargsian, the Defense Minister, one of the closest and most trusted members of his inner circle; and Serge Sargsian, the former Defense Minister of Nagorno Karabagh, whom Ter-Petrossian had invited three years earlier to serve in the same capacity in Armenia and who was later entrusted with the ministry of security and, in 1996, with the combined ministries of interior and security.

There seems to be some doubt on the constitutionality of the circumstances of the resignation. Following the resignation, Kocharian and Vazgen Sargsian expressed their belief that all was constitutional. In his resignation statement Ter-Petrossian carefully avoided characterizing the situation as unconstitutional, but he did specify that the exercise of his constitutional prerogatives, that is, the dismissal of cabinet members who defied the President's constitutional authority to set foreign and security policy, presented a serious danger of destabilizing the country. The normal course of action for subordinates who disagree with their President on substantial issues and whom they failed to convince to change course would have been, of course, to resign themselves.

The Constitutional Court was not apprised of the issue of the constitutionality of the resignation process by any of the parties. Most opinions expressed in Armenia were largely politically motivated and did not reflect serious considerations of constitutional law, which remains in its infancy in Armenia. In the absence of knowledge of the exact discussions that transpired between Ter-Petrossian and his antagonists, it is difficult to say more than the following: The process seems to have technically followed the constitutional order, but doubts remain whether the spirit of the Constitution was respected. By resigning, Ter-Petrossian avoided a constitutional crisis and a potentially disastrous confrontation.

The question of the constitutionality of the resignation remained irrelevant to important elements within the conventional opposition that had never recognized and/or liked the current Constitution. This is not to say that they liked the way the resignation was brought about, however much they welcomed the departure of Ter-Petrossian. Their nonrecognition of the Constitution of 1995 and of results of the 1996 presidential elections deprived them of arguments against Kocharian based on constitutional norms.

While the process that led to Ter-Petrossian's resignation was internal, that is, the actors and their motivations were primarily domestic to the Armenian scene, one cannot underestimate the importance of external forces and factors that, for different, even opposing reasons, weakened Ter-Petrossian's position and credibility. These forces had their own scenario as to who should be governing Armenia and how the conflict should proceed. The external forces strengthened the belief among Ter-Petrossian's antagonists that the international community would accept a viable alternative leadership. This book does not cover that aspect of the President's resignation. It is worth stating, nonetheless, that when that history is written, it will reveal some strange bedfellows.

Ter-Petrossian's resignation was explained through patent formulas, articulated quickly, that still constitute conventional wisdom on the subject. This conventional wisdom asserted that:

1. Ter-Petrossian had unexpectedly decided to accept a formula for the solution of the Karabagh conflict that was unacceptable to important members of his administration;

2. The move on the part of the antagonists came at that particular time because the position and proposed formula must have been new to them;

3. Ter-Petrossian accepted the formula as a result of excessive pressure from other countries and the mediators, the Co-Chairmen of the OSCE Minsk group, representing Russia, the United States, and France;

4. The substance of the difference between Ter-Petrossian and his antagonists consisted of the "step-by-step" as opposed to the "package-deal" approach; and,

5. In forcing the President's hand, the antagonists had the support of the Armenian people who favored a hard position on the conflict and considered his concessions defeatist if not treacherous.

It is interesting to note that in interviews following Ter-Petrossian's resignation, Kocharian has occasionally argued that the differences on the resolution of the conflict were not the only reason for the action of his group. That too is very much part of the debate and is addressed later.

BEYOND THE CONVENTIONAL WISDOM

Now that the dust has settled and the pundits have exhausted the subject, it is possible to look at those assertions and, based on largely public information, set some of the record straight. We will be able to see the larger issues behind the resignation. This is a useful exercise not in order to defend Ter-Petrossian, but because the erroneous identification of the problem will mislead policymakers and the interested communities—academic or otherwise—into raising false hopes and making the wrong judgment calls in the future, as has happened more than once in the past.

Whether or not one liked his personality or agreed with his policies, Ter-Petrossian would have to be considered the dominant figure of Armenia's history during the last decade. He was, possibly with Vazgen Manukian, the intellectual leader of the "Karabagh Committee," which, beginning in 1988, defended the rights of Karabagh Armenians and ended up leading Armenia to independence. In July 1990 Ter-Petrossian was elected President of the Supreme Soviet of a still Soviet Armenia, and in October 1991 he was elected the first executive-style President of independent Armenia. At the time of his resignation, he was serving the second year of his second five-year term.

Ter-Petrossian's vision shaped Armenia's transitional period to democracy, a free market economy and, most important, to a non-traditional foreign policy. In state building, he oversaw the institutional development of the National Assembly, the Presidency, the Constitution and Constitutional Court, and the armed forces; and he redefined the role of government and of relations between government and the citizen. He initiated reforms in the judiciary, health care, education, and social security. He also charted the path for the resolution of the Nagorno Karabagh conflict. Given the multiplicity of fronts in which change was needed and their inter-relatedness, Ter-Petrossian's basic philosophy of government was evolutionary, rather than revolutionary. Real social change was possible and would be evident, he argued, only with the gradual buildup of institutions and economic strength, both of which would enable reformist policies to take root.

Ter-Petrossian has had serious opposition and many detractors; he has invited more than his share of the usual hatred and jealousies. His opponents included the communists and extreme nationalists, as well as some former comrades-in-arms. There was domestic and international criticism regarding the handling of the 1995 parliamentary and 1996 presidential elections. Some people criticized him for being too tolerant and democratic; others considered him authoritarian or even dictatorial. His decision to resign invites further thinking on the subject of his relationship with power and office.

As a sitting president, he was naturally held responsible for everything that went wrong. For some of his detractors, nothing he did was right and everything he did was evil. Usually a man of few words, Ter-Petrossian expressed himself even less about such judgments.

Time and history will tell if his leadership during the period of transition was wise, if the state institutions he helped will survive, and if any of the reforms he initiated or policies he instituted were successful. Meanwhile, Ter-Petrossian has kept silent on these issues, giving tenuous credibility to any and all explanations and answers.

A careful look at what is in the public domain and avoidance of selective memory are sufficient to show that, at least regarding the issue of resignation, much that has been written is contrary to the evidence regarding the circumstances of the conflict between him and his close associates.

The truncated debate on Ter-Petrossian's resignation raises the following questions:

1. *Did Ter-Petrossian project a new flexibility during his 26 September 1997 press conference that in turn triggered the reaction of his associates?*

Ter-Petrossian's September 26 statement on the need for a compromise solution to the Nagorno Karabagh conflict contained nothing new. Ter-Petrossian had maintained the same position throughout his presidency and articulated it clearly both privately and publicly on many occasions. His refusal to recognize Nagorno Karabagh's unilateral declaration of independence in 1992, despite street protests and the popularity that such recognition would have brought him, is only one articulation of his long-held views on the resolution of the conflict.

The novelty was the public, coordinated, and even ferocious reaction of his close associates to that act of reiteration, a reaction that became even more pronounced in November, when, in response to the criticisms, Ter-Petrossian authored his famous "War or Peace" article.

Without discussing the choices available, in that article Ter-Petrossian revealed aspects of his reasoning as to why a compromise solution was necessary. Even then he did not reveal the outline, let alone the details, of the Proposal by the OSCE Minsk Group Co-Chairmen that he accepted as a basis for negotiations and that the others were rejecting.

2. Was there anything new for the antagonists in Ter-Petrossian's position?

Even if for the public there were some novelties in his statements in September and November, to his close associates none of it was new. They had all known that Ter-Petrossian had accepted the first draft of the same proposal presented the previous May by the mediators as a basis for negotiations, albeit with "serious reservations." He also had the second draft, presented in July. He did the same with the third and, if anything, in many ways much-improved draft of the same proposal that the mediators offered on September 22–23. Whether adequate or not, the changes the mediators introduced in the third draft addressed many of the concerns of the Armenian side, thus making it more, rather than less, acceptable to him.

Ter-Petrossian's colleagues also knew the full contents of all three draft proposals, which had remained the subject of intense and regular discussions between May and September. The public too knew of Ter-Petrossian's acceptance through formal statements, although they did not know the exact or full contents of the proposals. What details the Armenian citizen knew were mostly inaccurate, incomplete, and distorted bits and pieces, leaked largely by Baku for the purpose of selling the proposal to the Azerbaijani public and making it look like a diplomatic victory for Azerbaijan, which it certainly was not.

3. Was the essence of the disagreement between Ter-Petrossian and his associates turned antagonists related to the "step-by-step" as opposed to the "package-deal" approaches?

Until December 1996, the issues related to Karabagh were divided into two categories. The first set was grouped under "military-technical" issues or "the removal of the consequences of war," including the end of the blockades; the question of the return of occupied territories on both sides; the return of displaced persons and refugees, also on both sides; measures to strengthen the cease-fire; and other humanitarian issues, such as hostages and prisoners of war. These issues would be defined as the Karabagh *conflict*.

The second category refers to the question of the future status of Nagorno Karabagh and related issues. This is known as the *problem* of Karabagh. The "step-by-step" approach refers to a methodology of first negotiating one category of issues and implementing the solutions related to that category, and later on tackling the second category of issues. The "package-deal" approach refers to a process of negotiations where both sets of issues would be tackled simultaneously, possibly making the implementation of any agreement of one conditional on agreement on the other.

As understood in the context of the history of Karabagh negotiations, the "step-by-step" approach calls on negotiations in the first category of issues. An agreement "eliminating the consequences of war" would bring peace, that is, parties would permanently renounce the use of force. The status question would be resolved solely through negotiations, following the first phase. It constitutes the "land-for-peace" approach: Return of occupied territories—certainly not all—in return for all parties renouncing the use of force to settle what remains to be solved. The "package deal" would amount to what is known in other conflicts as "land for status." Occupied territories are regarded as the most valuable bargaining chips to secure the status preferred by those holding occupied territories.

OSCE Minsk Group negotiations, which began in June 1992 and reached a stalemate by the end of 1996, were based on the "step-by-step" approach: The problem of the status had not been discussed there. On many occasions the Karabagh delegation, which was a full participant in the Minsk Group negotiations, had requested that the Minsk Group also discuss the status question, which had immediately brought a demand by Azerbaijan and the other nine countries (not Armenia) that the Armenian side first recognize the principle of territorial integrity for Azerbaijan.

Despite the fact that the status had not been discussed during Minsk Group meetings, the Minsk Group Co-Chairmen—Russia, France, and the United States since 1997—offered to the parties three consecutive draft proposals in 1997 (May, July, and September)—the first two were based on the "package-deal" approach. They included a proposal for the status of Karabagh. Both proposed a dual track negotiation, one dealing with each category, with the proviso that the implementation of an agreement in one would not wait for the successful conclusion of negotiations on the other.

Ter-Petrossian had no ideological or principled opposition to either methodology. Yerevan had accepted with serious reservations the first two proposals as bases for negotiations and had rejected the inclusion of territorial integrity as a starting point for negotiations on the status. Baku stated that it had accepted them but with such reservations that the acceptance amounted to a rejection. Stepanakert rejected these two "packag-deal"-based drafts outright. There were even hints that it did not like the "package-deal" approach.

It was clear in July 1997 that the proposals were too ambitious to constitute a basis of negotiations and to produce real progress. It would be hard to reach a common denominator on so many issues, including the most complex, the future status of Karabagh. Given the impossibility of finding a formula to deal with the status issue, the Co-Chairmen then dropped the section dealing with the status in the third draft proposal presented in September.

Once Azerbaijan and Nagorno Karabagh practically rejected the first two drafts, Ter-Petrossian was even more convinced that an agreement on the status was out of reach for the time being; that insistence on status at this time would paralyze the negotiations and any progress made so far in the resolution of the conflict; and that the "step-by-step" approach, if coupled with the necessary security guarantees for the territory and people of Nagorno Karabagh, was the best approach.

What, in fact, had been lost in the complexity of texts was also a third category, but one more important than the others is some respects: The security guarantees for the people and territory of Karabagh, regardless of status and regardless of what portion of the occupied territories would be returned. In the May and July draft proposals, security guarantees were dispersed in the two parts of the proposals and remained unsatisfactory. On the insistence of Yerevan, and with much labor, the Co-Chairmen grouped the security guarantees in a new "basket" and incorporated it in the third version, including some elements that they had not accepted before or that had not been incorporated into the proposal. The status question was eliminated from the proposal.

Thus, had the September "step-by-step" proposal been accepted by all as a basis of negotiations and had negotiations on the text been successful, the following would have been the likely situation:

A. Peace would come to Karabagh, Armenia, and Azerbaijan, in return for occupied territories that had no bearing on the security issue. Talk of Shushi or Lachin being returned to Azerbaijan on the basis of this agreement amounted to Azeri propaganda and false accusations by Ter-Petrossian opponents. The proposal had no mention of the return of either. President Aliyev of Azerbaijan had made the concession on Lachin while visiting Washington in the summer of 1997, agreeing to relegate its final solution to the phase of negotiations on the status of Karabagh. Shushi was mentioned in passing, certainly not as territory to be returned.

B. The insistence on the principle of territorial integrity (supported by Azerbaijan and the international community, supported by every single member of the OSCE and every "friend" of Armenia, including Russia, Iran, and others), which had won the day over the principle of the self-determination of peoples (supported by Armenia and Karabagh) had been eliminated from the proposal with the elimination of the discussion of status. This meant that the 1996 OSCE Lisbon Summit statement, which had listed that principle as the first point, had been reversed de facto.

C. Until such time as final status negotiations produced a mutually acceptable treaty, Karabagh would keep its current status. That meant that Karabagh would remain de facto independent of Azerbaijan, and its existing relations with Armenia would not be reversed.

D. Security guarantees for Karabagh and its people would go into effect immediately, before the final status was agreed on.

It is possible that Karabagh leaders and Ter-Petrossian's former associates were not satisfied with the security guarantees or with any other major or minor point in the September proposal. Without going into details, it is important to point out that, first, Ter-Petrossian considered the security guarantees adequate, and some refinement would have been introduced during negotiations; second, a number of the points would still have to be improved, but that is the purpose of negotiations.

Nonetheless, the disagreement was said to be about methodology rather than specifics: The "package-deal" as opposed to the "step-by-step" approach.

Yet, Kocharian was Chairman of Karabagh's State Defense Council and later President of Nagorno Karabagh during most of the OSCE Minsk Group negotiations, which were based exclusively on the "step-by-step" approach; Vazgen Sargsian was Defense Minister, then State Minister, then again Defense Minister during the entire period; Serge Sargsian was Defense Minister of Nagorno Karabagh, then of Armenia, then Minister of Interior and Security of Armenia, during the same period. Robert Kocharian was Prime Minister of Armenia when Ter-Petrossian accepted the first two proposals in May and July 1997, which could have been construed as representing either methodology, but which Karabagh rejected.

If the problem for Ter-Petrossian's associates-turned-antagonists was the proposal's methodology, that is, their insistence on a "package deal," they would have worked hard to have the May or July draft transformed into a more acceptable basis for negotiations. That had not happened.

4. *Did Ter-Petrossian accept the OSCE draft proposal as a basis for negotiations because of excessive pressure on him from the international community?*

Contrary to general belief, including that of some international commentators, the OSCE mediators did not exert unusual pressure on Ter-Petrossian in 1997. In fact, compared to some of the other instances during the five years of OSCE-led negotiations, the mediators—Russia, the United States, and France—functioned in a cooperative, collegial, and constructive manner among themselves and with the parties to the conflict. Furthermore, especially in September, the efforts of the mediators were directed at the restart of the negotiations, not at the acceptance by the parties of the draft proposal. There was always opportunity at the end to refuse a text one did not like.

Ter-Petrossian had often refused proposals before, but he had always countered them with his own initiatives and ideas. On the one hand, he refused to recognize Nagorno Karabagh's unilateral declaration of independence, believing that any lasting peace should be the outcome of negotiations, that is, the solution and the compromises each party must make would have to be acceptable to the parties involved. On the other hand, he also resisted the tremendous pressure of the collective OSCE and its individual countries and was not reluctant to veto the counter-productive OSCE Lisbon Summit statement in 1996. One reason for his veto was that the statement was not the product of negotiations among all parties concerned.

I believe Ter-Petrossian accepted the September Proposal as a basis of negotiations because (a) he liked what he saw, (b) the mediators had made a serious effort to accommodate the legitimate concerns of the parties, and (c) negotiations within the Minsk Group that were to follow the parties' acceptance of the draft proposal as a basis for discussions provided a venue for further refining and adjusting the document.

5. *Did the people of Armenia oppose Ter-Petrossian's solution, and was the opposition of the Kocharian-led group a reflection of the popular will?*

The assertion that the people of Armenia opposed Ter-Petrossian's approach is not based on any factual evidence. Since the beginning of the national movement ten years ago, the people of Armenia have shown extraordinary resilience and circumspection. Their votes indicate support for caution and moderation.

In fact, the "people" had very little to do with the latest events. There was no referendum on the issue; and the debate on alternative solutions, in which Ter-Petrossian invited his opponents to engage in before his resignation, never materialized.

It is hard to say what the people of Armenia would have opted for, had they been given the choice. A debate on that specific proposal would have been difficult anyway. As stated earlier, neither Ter-Petrossian nor his antagonists revealed its contents. The former President may be faulted for this. He alone can explain his strategy. But one can venture two comments. First, unlike President Aliyev of Azerbaijan, Ter-Petrossian felt bound by the ground rules of the negotiations, which required confidentiality. Additionally, he did not think it was proper to present the details of a proposal that was still a proposal and had not been negotiated by the parties. But a debate of how each party, group, or politician would resolve the conflict and the problem, independent of the particulars of the draft proposal on hand, was possible. Unfortunately, however, that debate did not take place.

Ter-Petrossian can be faulted too for the strategy he adopted to achieve a consensus on a plan that required difficult choices and that could easily be exploited by demagogues. He envisioned a rational process to reach a decision, as for so many other difficult choices. He first gathered and assessed information and relevant factors; then, he thought through as many aspects of a problem as he could; third, he engaged in intensive debate with associates formally and/or informally, in a style that encouraged all differences to be aired and debated; finally came the decision, by consensus, when possible, but always a decision for which he could and would take responsibility.

The decision-making process on the most critical of problems facing the country required intellectual strength, ability to argue and convince, readiness to listen and to be convinced with rational arguments as well as strength of character and an ever-present sense of the larger picture. These traits made possible the transcending of traditional thinking and gave Ter-Petrossian the power of conviction, including conviction in the rational process and in his solution to the problem. But these same traits came to be seen as his weaknesses: an intellectual aloofness at the expense of public relations and political expediency, rigidity with his adversaries, and unwillingness to compromise for the sake of staying in power.

Some people have termed this a problem of communication. The curious thing is that Ter-Petrossian was an excellent communicator—when he decided to communicate, that is. Otherwise, he would not have been propelled from his position as a senior researcher at the Library of Ancient Manuscripts to membership in the Karabagh Committee and its intellectual leadership and, ultimately, to the leadership of the country. Contrary to Soviet jargon or ideological and nationalistic rhetoric, he spoke clearly and articulated ideas succinctly, using as few words as possible. Language—and what it changed in people—was his preferred weapon not only against the Soviet solution to the Karabagh problem but also against that abhorrence called the "Soviet Man" speaking in "Sovietese." He respected words, believed in their intrinsic value and in the ability of citizens to make judgments, and sought to restore their power in order to bring about real communication. That may have been one important reason he was so frugal with words. The doubts about the impact of his policies and the legitimacy of his power had not diminished the respect that people had for his rare statements—they listened carefully when he talked—and about their belief that he was expressing what he believed to be the problem or situation. He distilled his ideas before offering them and expressed them clearly and in simple, even harsh, terms.

The problem is that he decided not to reveal all the factors relevant to the debate. His November 1997 article "War or Peace" provided just the bottom line. He certainly did not reveal major points of the proposal or their significance. It is not self-evident that simply doing so would have would succeeded in the acceptance of his policy and saved his presidency. It may have been too late.

Above and beyond all that was said and left unsaid, all that was done or could have been done but was not done, had there been a way to have a referendum and debate, had they been given all the relevant facts and assessments, I believe the people of Armenia would have voted with a clear majority, even if not overwhelmingly, in favor of Ter-Petrossian's solution. At any rate, the Ter-Petrossian solution to the conflict would have received more votes than did Ter-Petrossian the candidate during the second presidential elections in 1996.

We may never know. But let us consider the official figures of the 1998 presidential elections. Having removed the sitting President on the question of Karabagh and enjoying the support of hard-liners, including the Interior and Defense Ministers as well as the ARF and other parties, Kocharian received only 40 percent of the popular vote on the first-round of the presidential election. Karen Demirjian, with hardly an organization on his side, managed 30 percent, overshadowing all others, including Vazgen Manukian. In the second-round, Demirjian managed to receive 40 percent or more votes, despite the handicaps related to his past status and despite Kocharian's advantage as Acting President. As stated earlier, the question of Karabagh did not emerge as a campaign issue for either candidate. But Demirjian, in response to a reporter's question on how he would resolve the conflict, answered that he knew President Heydar Aliyev of Azerbaijan personally (when Aliyev was First Secretary of Azerbaijan's Communist Party and subsequently a member of the USSR Communist Party Politburo) and he was sure that could be an advantage in finding a solution. It would be hard to characterize that statement as a "hard line" on Karabagh; it is closer to an invitation to a compromise solution. At a minimum, it was not a condemnation of the Ter-Petrossian approach. To interpret the votes Demirjian received as the "nostalgia" vote is to show a lack of respect for the ability of the Armenian voter to understand issues and personalities. Whatever else one may say about the citizens of Armenia, for the most part they shun extremes and instability and have respect for circumspection and caution.

I cannot argue that the people of Karabagh would have voted in favor of such a resolution. Armenians in that long-isolated area have evolved a historically different political culture. In addition, a siege mentality and a militarized environment, fostered by Azerbaijan's policies before and after the dissolution of the USSR, have made them more weary of any solution less than total union with Armenia. These same circumstances also give the leadership a quasi-monopolistic control over the debate on any proposal and on its outcome.

A MATTER OF ECONOMICS?

If the particulars presented here do not support the conventional view of the circumstances of the Ter-Petrossian resignation, can one seek an answer elsewhere?

First, it should be stated clearly and unequivocally that the existing differences about the solution to the problem do not signal the cowardice of one and the courage of the other. Moralistic terminology constitutes escape from an obligation to present solutions and strategies and to take the responsibility for their consequences.

Nagorno Karabagh and its people are dear to every Armenian; Karabagh's future is of concern to all; it will affect every Armenian, though in different ways and to varying degrees. Any solution will affect most closely the people who are living there and the people of Armenia, and in a much less practical way the Armenians of the Diaspora.

The pan-national character of the problem places great responsibility on everyone who wishes to have an impact on its solution, from near and far, but especially on those who are in a position to make decisions on the various choices, as long as choices are still available. Kocharian and the leaders of Karabagh have all stated on more than one occasion that they are ready to accept compromises.

Speaking strictly of Ter-Petrossian and Kocharian, their differences lie in the kind of compromise that is acceptable to one or the other and, even more significantly, in the timing of any compromise and in the assessment each man gave to the strengths and weaknesses of the Armenian side relative to Azerbaijan. For, beyond the conflict, there still was one problem: the economic and social well-being of the Armenian people in Armenia and in Karabagh—poverty, unemployment, low wages, and attendant social problems.

As became clear in the statements of the two leaders and in the subsequent debate, however muffled, each man had a different view of the relationship between the conflict, on the one hand, and the social-economic situation in the land, including Karabagh, on the other. Since the cease-fire, which was first signed as a temporary agreement in May 1994 but was transformed into a permanent one in July and August of the same year, the debate within and between the administrations of Armenia and Karabagh had begun to shift gradually.

The new questions were these: To what extent were the conflict, accompanying blockades, and "no war but no peace" environment responsible for the lack of economic development and growth? Is the economy a factor in the timing of concessions? Is time with or against the Armenian side?

Ter-Petrossian's arguments can be summarized in the following way. The blockades by Azerbaijan and Turkey and the absence of peace were stifling Armenia's economic development and foreign investments; they were an obstacle to Armenia's ability to be part of and keep pace with regional developments; they would continue to sap the budget. There were concessions that could have been made in 1997 without endangering the future and security of the people and land of Karabagh. Regardless of formulas and slogans, the Armenian side was likely to make concessions in the future, the differences being more symbolic than real. Time was not with the Armenian side, regardless of developments in Azerbaijan. The relative advantages the Armenian side presently had in negotiations in 1997 may not be there in the future.

Kocharian argued that while the conflict and related circumstances were factors in explaining the social-economic situation in the land, they did not constitute the essential reason for the lack of economic development. More important factors included the lack of strong management and discipline within the government, corruption, Ter-Petrossian's inability to co-opt the opposition in the national struggle, his divisive politics, and ineffective and uneasy relations with the Diaspora. Kocharian proposed that with better management, more discipline, a strong anticorruption policy, a forceful effort to achieve unity, and the coordination of the resources of the state of Armenia and the Diaspora, the Armenian side could both improve its economic performance sufficiently to lift the majority of its population out of poverty and give it time to wait for a more propitious moment to deal with the Nagorno Karabagh problem. He also thought that diplomatic isolation could be broken through a more aggressive diplomacy that would win support from the international community for the least concession. Kocharian believed that given the geopolitical dangers of oil for Azerbaijan and the problems of an inherently corrupt system there, time was not on Azerbaijan's side.

Ter-Petrossian too believed that the economy had more room for development and that all the factors listed by Kocharian were important and relevant. He was convinced, however, that even the best efforts and maximum results in all these areas would not be sufficient to bring a qualitatively significant change in the standard of living of the people. Furthermore, however much he may have agreed with his then Prime Minister that Armenia could improve its diplomatic performance, Ter-Petrossian could not see how Armenian or any other diplomacy could change the position of other countries on territorial integrity and occupied territories. In other words, he could not see a change in the positions of these countries, including the "friends of Armenia," whose policies were based on their own national interests and who had their own actual or potential Karabaghs. Russia had Chechnya and many other potential Chechnyas; Greece had Cyprus and the Aegean islands; Iran had its "Southern Azerbaijan"; and even France had its Corsica. Moreover, in the post-Soviet geopolitical space, whether rightly or wrongly, the international community saw in territorial integrity a valued principle of international security and stability.

Kocharian and his associates, including the leadership Kocharian left behind in Karabagh, considered the war won; should there be another round of fighting, that too would be won. They believed negotiations should consolidate the victory and give Armenians time to cash in.

Ter-Petrossian thought that war was not just a series of battles, and not just about heroes; it was more than victories, and it was not over. War included economy, psychology, and soldiers supported by their families. Time could change the equation, with no guarantees that the Armenian hand would then be stronger in relation to Azerbaijan.

This did not mean, in Ter-Petrossian's view, that Azerbaijan's policies of economic strangulation (with Turkey's own supportive blockade) and of diplomatic isolation of Armenia could break the will of Armenians to defend the rights of Nagorno Karabagh. No economic hardship could alter the view shared by all Armenians that history should not be repeated: no more deportations, no more genocide.

I believe Ter-Petrossian invited Kocharian to serve as Armenia's Prime Minister in March 1997 to give him an opportunity to prove his point. Kocharian now had authority over and responsibility for the economic and social spheres. Ter-Petrossian remained the arbiter in cases of disputes within the government and continued to determine foreign policy and the course of negotiations.

By September 1997, after six months with his new Prime Minister, Ter-Petrossian might have been more convinced than ever that he was right, as economic indicators did not show signs of significant improvement. Kocharian, in turn, is likely to have concluded, rightly or wrongly, that his powers were not sufficient to prove his point, and that any concessions on Nagorno Karabagh while he was trying to vindicate his analysis were uncalled for.

There is a very curious phenomenon, which is hardly unique to Armenian political culture. When confronted with failure or the possibility of failure, many highly placed officials of the administration have explained their partial or total failure by their inability to impact developments and decisions in areas beyond their jurisdiction, that is, by arguing that they do not or did not have enough power. Few have questioned their own assumptions, management, or capabilities. This symptom may explain the large number of candidates for the presidency from the ranks of former officials of the Ter-Petrossian administrations: former Prime Minister Vazgen Manukian; former senior presidential adviser Ashot Manucharian; Hrand Bagratian, the Prime Minister with the longest tenure under Ter-Petrossian; former Minister of Security and Karabagh negotiator Davit Shahnazarian.

I am not discounting serious policy differences; the country is facing so many critical issues that it is normal for allies to develop serious differences on existing or emerging issues. Nor is there anything wrong with citizens and politicians seeking the presidency. In fact, it is a positive sign. But the symptom also tends to cover up failures of policies and personal failings.

Kocharian had not necessarily failed. Six months are too short to make a judgment, although when he accepted the position of Prime Minister he himself asked the press for six months to show what difference his management would make. That was in March 1997. The public wrangling over the OSCE proposals began with the September proposal, and not with the May or July drafts. At the least, Kocharian must have realized that moving the economy was not as easy as he thought. Yerevan was not Stepanakert, in more ways than one. He must have also concluded that Ter-Petrossian's continuing involvement in domestic and foreign affairs was a hindrance to the manner in which he wanted to proceed. Time may clarify the degree to which, if at all, the drive to have full control was a significant factor in explaining Kocharian's move.

One does not need more time, however, to assess the importance of the economy both in Armenia's politics and for its politicians, as well as Karabagh's significance in Armenia's domestic and foreign policies. One does not need more time to see how, for a small, impoverished, and landlocked country still technically at war, foreign and domestic policies are inextricably interwoven. The differences between Ter-Petrossian and Kocharian are more than a matter of quantitative analyses on growth rates and per capita income.

Ter-Petrossian's position was informed by his definition of the state and its mission, by his positions both on how to provide for Armenia's security and on the foreign policy principles that ensue from such security needs, and by the role he assigned to the conflict in his worldview. The events leading to Ter-Petrossian's resignation and what has happened since indicate that more than politics as usual, the political conflict is as much a clash of antagonistic worldviews and the role assigned to the Karabagh problem within each.

The question is, can Armenia and Karabagh risk such a clash that can turn violent or, even, can it afford politics as usual?

3.

Political Landscape II:
The Karabagh Problem
Revisited

A rmenia's politics has more than its share of paradoxes and inconsistencies.

Ter-Petrossian was compelled to resign because he accepted as a basis of negotiations a document that did not secure Karabagh the recognition of its independent status but also did not prejudge the territory's future status, did not recognize Azerbaijan's territorial integrity, precluded the use of force to impose a status unwanted by Karabagh, and left the possibility open for any solution, including independence. In 1998 President Kocharian and Ter-Petrossian's conventional opposition working with Kocharian accepted as a basis of negotiations a document that places Karabagh in a "common state" with Azerbaijan, a formula that is easily understood as a form of recognition of Azerbaijan's territorial integrity.

Some political parties had refused to recognize the legitimacy of the referendum on the Constitution, the National Assembly, and presidential elections in 1995 and 1996. When Ter-Petrossian was removed, these same parties suddenly granted legitimacy to the same Constitution, National Assembly, and officials elected under the Constitution. Two parties, the National Democratic Union (NDU) and the Armenian Revolutionay Federation (ARF), which insisted that the law be respected, reserved to themselves the right to violate it and to do so with impunity.

The report by the election monitors of the Organization for Security and Cooperation in Europe (OSCE) was considered evidence of election fraud in 1996, but a political act in 1998. Armenia's nonrecognition of Karabagh's independence constituted

"selling" Karabagh in 1992 but not in 1998. Seeking normalization of relations with Turkey without prior conditions by the Ter-
Petrossian administration was treason, but not so when advocated
by the Kocharian administration.

Ter-Petrossian's policies were considered "pro-Western," even
though excellent relations were developed with Iran and Russia,
including the first-ever major Treaty of Friendship and Cooperation with the latter. Strained diplomatic relations with both since
Ter-Petrossian's resignation are assessed as "excellent" and as
evidence of a sound foreign policy based on national interests.

It will be a relief if, at the end, time shows that these paradoxes
and inconsistencies constituted politics as usual, at which point
one could be tempted to argue that, once in power, parties and
politicians act more cautiously and responsibly. While this may
be true for some parties and politicians, in the case of others the
relativization of problems such as Karabagh, security, foreign
policy, the Constitution, and democracy raises the question of the
hierarchy of values and goals. What, at the end, is important to
the players? What is the world within which these shifts and
inconsistencies make sense?

Even if the purpose of a political party or a politician is to
achieve power, how does each see the role of the state it wants to
lead? And, finally, how does Karabagh, fit into all of this? What
is the problem of Karabagh, or what is the problem each party or
politician is trying to resolve through Karabagh?

PRAGMATISTS AND VISIONARIES

Within a year of independence, Armenia's political life was filled
with parties that represented all the shades of the spectrum from
extreme right to extreme left, if one were to use the traditional terminology. But a particular kind of struggle provided the under-
current of the political battles throughout Ter-Petrossian's tenure.
At times transparent and mostly unstated, the antagonism reached
the level of "schisms," reminiscent of theological debates in the
fourth and fifth centuries.

Ter-Petrossian and the Armenian National Movement (ANM)
represented the core of the first camp and promoted one world-

view: to bring normalcy to Armenia and to the Armenian people, transcend its tortured past, avoid ideological constraints, and follow a pragmatic route. This group included a number of politicians and groups that distanced themselves from the ANM and Ter-Petrossian on specific issues but that still share, in my view, the basic tenets: Hrand Bagratian, Prime Minister under Ter-Petrossian (1993–1996); Davit Shahnazarian, former Minister of Security and adviser to Ter-Petrossian, who has remained an independent political figure; Edvard Yegorian, member of Parliament, who organized the "Hayrenik" (Fatherland) faction in Parliament once he left the ANM; and others.

The second camp ascribed to Armenia and the Armenian nation the role of achieving a "higher" vision, ideal, mission, or status. Each in its own way, Vazgen Manukian's National Democratic Union (NDU), the Armenian Revolutionary Federation (ARF), the Communist Party of Armenia (CPA), and the Democratic Party of Armenia (DPA) extolled a "national ideology" that, even if left undefined, assigned the Armenian state and its people a pre-ordained role beyond the one the people would assign it.

These two divergent and increasingly opposing visions of the place of Armenia and Armenians on earth overshadowed what normal discourse did take place. The fierce struggle for the soul of Armenia, as the ideologists saw it, could not but engender intolerance and personal hatred of the heretic who personified the lack of national ideology, Levon Ter-Petrossian.

Ter-Petrossian and the ANM

For Ter-Petrossian and the ANM, the purpose of statehood was to ensure that the citizens of Armenia could define their own interests, agenda, and strategy in order to achieve security. Statehood was the mechanism through which the inhabitants of that land secure their rightful place in the world community, a means by which they determine their own problems, define their own national interests, and pursue these interests as they see fit. The purposes of government are to provide for the security of the land and its people, to ensure conditions that bring about the well-being—political, economic, and social—of citizens, and to resolve problems that threaten or undermine these goals. The transformation of society and the securing of the people's well-being required time; they were best guaranteed when implemented with deliberation; no revolutionary act, ideology, or regime could create instant economic development or functioning institutions. Ideological fervor could not replace time; overzealous nationalism could be no substitute for circumspection. The purpose of independence was to enable the people of Armenia to feel and act as normal nations do.

Ter-Petrossian and the ANM sought the guarantee for Armenia's independence in a balanced foreign policy and its ultimate security in good relations with all its neighbors. Normalization of relations with Turkey was part of this pragmatic foreign policy as well as a precondition for the normalization of the nation's life. Until such time as normal relations were established with all four neighbors and a new security structure was in place, Armenia would seek security guarantees elsewhere, as it did with Russia in 1997.

For the ANM, the substance of the problem of Karabagh consisted of the security and collective rights of the people of Karabagh. In 1988 these rights were pursued through the goal of unification with Armenia. By 1992 that goal was adjusted to post-Soviet realities. Karabagh was one of Armenia's challenges, albeit a very special and critical one. Neither its substance nor the strategy of a solution could be defined or pursued independently of the realities of Armenia. Ter-Petrossian argued that an economically, socially, and politically weak and diplomatically isolated Armenia would be altogether useless for the defense of the territory or people of Karabagh.

For the ANM and Ter-Petrossian, the war in Karabagh was thrust on Karabagh and Armenia, and it had to be won because no government of Armenia could accept a new genocide or deportations. But once their defense had been secured, the problem had to be resolved in order to give both Armenia and Karabagh a chance to achieve normalcy.

Thus, the war of Karabagh was a defensive war, and not a war of expansion. Armenia did not seek territorial aggrandizement in general. The problem of Karabagh had to be resolved within the bounds of international law, on the basis of Karabagh's vital interests, and not on formalistic or symbolic advantages.

Ter-Petrossian considered a peace agreement crucial to creating the political, economic, and social bases for the consolidation of reforms and independence. For that he was ready to accept a solution based on mutual compromises by the Azerbaijani and Armenian sides, which secured a status that precluded Karabagh's domination by Azerbaijan and effective security guarantees, including boundary adjustments that made Karabagh contiguous with Armenia. This solution was not everything others may wish for, but it was everything Karabagh needed.

The return of occupied territory not necessary for Karabagh's security link with Armenia would be the means to achieve that peace agreement. A peace agreement without an agreement on status was acceptable because, in fact, it left intact Karabagh's de facto status: independent of Azerbaijan and quasi-integrated with Armenia.

A timely resolution of the conflict would also end Armenia's blockades, opening up its communications and transport routes, and thus allowing it to play a role in regional and transcontinental links and ending the assessment of most foreign investors as a risky and insecure area. The timely resolution of the Karabagh conflict would also ensure normal relations with two of the four neighbors and would alleviate strain from the relations with the two others, Iran and Georgia, as well as from the rest of the international community.

There remained the crucial matter of the relationship of the state with Armenians living beyond its borders. Was the Armenian state a conventional state belonging to its citizens or was it "home" for all Armenians, regardless of where they resided and of which country they were citizens? Was an Armenian government responsible to all Armenians, their wishes and dreams? What, at the end, constitutes an Armenian?

For the ANM and Ter-Petrossian, the state would take responsibility for those issues it considered essential to its interests and for those issues of the nation living within its boundaries. The state also brings, within the limits of international law, its own contribution to the protection of the interests and needs of Armenians in other countries. However, Armenians living outside the country's boundaries, except for the particular circumstances of Karabagh and its inhabitants, were part of the Armenian nation in a nonlegal way. Armenians constituted one nation historically and to some extent culturally, even spiritually. Legally, however, Diasporans were citizens of other countries. They had the option to return to the homeland and to enjoy the full benefits—and assume the full responsibilities—of citizenship. But it was utopian, even dangerous, to disregard the legal distinctions. The two parts of the nation had much to give to each other, but relations should be based on mutual respect and on the recognition of differences.

This was the worldview. This view does not constitute a list of achievements. The worldview represents the context within which problems were seen and major policy decisions were made; it does not ensure that every official acted altruistically on every occasion or strictly within the bounds of this ideal, nor does it explain away the failures, personal and political, that undermined the policies and the trust of the people toward the ANM and, ultimately, toward Ter-Petrossian. But failures do not diminish the role of this worldview in understanding the direction in which Armenia was heading under Ter-Petrossian and the antagonism toward the values and goals it represented.

The Conventional Opposition

Politics for this group of parties is the mechanism that is managed in a manner so as to achieve a higher vision or ideal. Within this worldview, the state plays a predetermined role as the main vehicle for the realization of that higher ideal. Politics neither begins nor ends with the people and their needs as defined by the people. Here, the people are expected to behave in a manner consistent with the script prepared by the visionary, a script that will elevate the people and make them conform to the role assigned to them within the vision. Ideologically based worldviews are not uncommon in history or in the contemporary world. They are, after all, the stuff of which totalitarianism regimes are made.

A. Vazgen Manukian and the NDU

The most serious difference between Ter-Petrossian and Vazgen Manukian revolves around the word *normalcy*. Manukian believes that to base a whole philosophy of state on that word means reducing the past, the present, and the future of Armenia and Armenians into an unacceptably limiting concept. Armenians, according to Manukian, have a higher mission, which emanates from the belief that Armenians are a special people, with an exceptional potential. The purposes of the state are to ensure that this potential is actualized and to find the arenas in which that mission may be made manifest.

Armenians are special by the power that could be derived from Armenia's history of oppression and pain, which can be turned into inner strength and which achieves miracles. Armenians are also special by the potential to achieve oneness: They feel or could come to feel one and must act as one, although a segment is in Armenia, another in Karabagh, and still others in dispersion. The state is the machine within which the oneness can be actualized, through which these disparate components of the same collective being can be marshaled and a new level of strength achieved that would secure the Armenian ideal at home and its special place on earth.

That strength was manifest in the war of Karabagh. Karabagh served as the arena in which a miracle was worked out. It showed that the "Armenian Cause" is achievable. Manukian believed in the value of the Armenian Cause, which explains his affinity with the ARF. As early as 1989, Manukian had discussed in an interview the validity of the quest for the recovery of Western Armenian territories. He had argued, however, that independence would have to precede that quest.

From Manukian's perspective, a Western-type democracy could not necessarily bring about the manifestation of Armenia's strength. The quest for "normalcy," argued Manukian, had reduced the people of Armenia to a "sleeping mass" lacking moral values and had turned the nation into despicable small shopkeepers going after their measly daily bread. Such a people could not feel the strength; they could not see what was good for them; they could not see the light. There was plenty of evidence for his scorn when the "people" did not respond adequately to his continuing calls to show their feelings by supporting him in the elections or did not respond to his call to "take matters into their own hands." No matter; Manukian could designate the 15,000 or 20,000 protesters gathered on 26 September 1996 as "the people" and could find other ways to articulate their "will" as manifested in his strength and determination to have the Parliament building occupied and its President kidnapped and beaten, just as a start. To wake up a lethargic nation, Manukian was prepared to deny Ter-Petrossian what the latter considered most precious for the country, its stability.

The key to change was to have the right leadership. Once that was achieved, the new Armenia and the rejuvenated Armenian nation would be strong enough to resolve the other problems, including Karabagh.

But it had to be the right leadership. Manukian argued that he was that person, the one person who feels the pain and suffering of his nation's history, the one who has the inner strength and determination to transform history, to elevate the nation from its downtrodden, corrupt, lazy, and demoralized state into a morally clean, efficient, energetic, productive and, of course, special nation.

If all of this sounds somewhat mystical and mysterious, that is because this particular worldview *is* both mysterious and mystical. As in the case of other guardians of visions of grandeur, the discourse defies rational debate.

No doubt the program envisions improvement in the lives of the citizens—a dramatic and quick improvement, at that. Yet it is difficult to translate a strategy based on intangibles, such as inner strength and inspiration, into budgets and laws. It would also be easy to avoid responsibility for failure if it is the people who failed to transform themselves into the kind of Armenians and citizens the program calls for. A government or leader whose program requires a different populace will always ask for more powers to bring about that transformation. Vazgen Manukian's relationship to power during his tenure as Prime Minister from 1990 to 1991 was only symptomatic of the pattern that such a worldview dictates.

B. The Communists

Armenian communists have never felt comfortable, confident, or secure in an independent Armenian state. For them, that is too lonely, too burdensome, too small a place. They would feel more at ease when performing a role in someone else's vision, someone who represents a higher, more universal idea or civilization. In this case, the purposes of the state are to find that someone, that state or empire, and to navigate toward its orbit.

Whether it is due to ideological inertia from the early days of inspired Armenian Bolshevik revolutionaries or to the kinds of people who are attracted to communistic parties today, the only constant in the thinking of communistic parties has been devotion to Russia. Whether tsarist Russia, Bolshevik Russia, Soviet Russia or the Russian Federation was insignificant, as long as it was an imperial Russia.

For the CPA led by Sergey Badalian, the DPA under Aram Sargsian, and other fellow travelers from the past and the present, security is found in the transfer of responsibilities—for domestic, foreign, and security policy—to Russia, always in the name of a higher ideal: building socialism, anti-imperialism, anti-Western culture. At the end, for these parties the cause of all problems must be sought in not having pleased Russia enough. Solutions will then be self-evident.

For the communistic parties, foreign policy under their rule would be simple. The Cold War was not dead, and Armenia will have made its choice. Armenia would know how to orient itself in world affairs. Even if the Cold War was dead, it is necessary to revive it, and communist ideology would know how to achieve that. The world is a rather simple place. Countries befriended by Russia would be Armenia's allies. Russia's enemies are Armenia's as well.

In this clearly defined world where one needs not make choices, Armenia's security problem would be automatically solved, because Armenia would be part of a larger entity. Trumpeting a slanted history and a future full of fear from the evil that Turkey represents would be sufficient to keep Armenia important for Russia's interests and to keep away nonpatriotic temptations, such as normalizing relations with Turkey, Russia's eternal enemy.

Running the economy would also be simple. Armenia could make tires for cars produced near Moscow; poverty and unemployment would disappear, as they did under Soviet rule. Social problems—corruption, prostitution, and the like—would disappear as well, by Party decree or by a vote of the Supreme Soviet.

Within this worldview, one would also find the strategy to solve the Karabagh problem. By uniting with Russia or joining the Russia-Belarus Union, Armenia would have proven its unquestioned loyalty to Russia. Once Armenia was part of Russia, Russia would reward it with Karabagh. It is, one must also admit, a simple solution. No diplomatic effort on the part of Armenia, no negotiations, no thinking or analysis, in fact, no effort at all would be needed.

One may argue that to achieve Karabagh's union with Armenia one may have had to sacrifice something, and Karabagh was important enough to sacrifice independence for it. In fact, part of the timidity with which Armenian communists and others approached the prospect of independence can be explained by their fear that such an act would be considered anti-Russian and would risk retaliation by Russia on Karabagh and, some would argue, on other territorial issues.

The argument was presented first in muted fashion, later on more overtly, by the communist parties, and was implied by other politicians. By 1996, encouraged by continuing social and economic hardships and by stalemate in Karabagh negotiations, the CPA collected signatures in support of Armenia's participation in the declared Russia-Belarus union.

The problem is that such logic has been tried consistently in history; it has not worked simply because scenarios written by Armenians have not always been the ones Russia decided to execute. The exchange has been a figment of some Armenians' imagination, predicated on their overeagerness to define Russian interests as the same as those of Armenia and Armenians.

History, unfortunately, has not supported this argument. No expression of love, from the beginning of Armenian-Russian relations in the eighteenth century through the Russian revolution and the formation of the USSR, seems to have been adequate to ensure that Armenian Karabagh came under Armenian control. From Stalin to Gorbachev, Russia's leaders have missed the opportunity to reciprocate and have awarded Karabagh to Azerbaijan.

British behavior was no different, incidentally, during the First Republic, when that Empire controlled Karabagh. General Andranik's admiration for the British—and his distrust of Russians—made no difference in the British policy in 1919 that aimed at placating Azerbaijan. In fact, it was judgment based on admiration and hatred that led to the national hero's decision to stop the march of his troops to Shushi at the request of the British, when Andranik's forces could have resolved that problem. France, too, behaved similarly in 1921, when it abandoned Cilicia to Turkey, despite its earlier promises to turn that region over to the local Armenians, who had fought on the side of France during the Great War.

Since the dissolution of the USSR, the administration of President Boris Yeltsin as well as its Communist opposition have reaffirmed their unmitigated support for the principle of territorial integrity, including that of Azerbaijan. Russia has always had its own way of defining its interests—once imperial, now national—which must include something more than a love affair with Armenians.

Regardless of the outcome, Armenian communistic parties are certain that the scenario requires that Communists be first given the reins of power in Armenia as the most reliable "pro-Russian" element. The rest of the issues would be details. Someone else could always be blamed for the loss of Karabagh. History would be written the way it was written for seventy years, and the Communists know how to deal with those who disagreed with their interpretation.

The issue here is not, of course, the kind of relations that Armenia should have with Russia. Rather, the issue is the manner in which such relations are perceived. There is no doubt that Armenia has common, including strategic, interests with Russia. That not all interests coincide is also true. The two states must cooperate, and they have done so since independence, by determining and pursuing those common interests and, based on mutual respect, by disagreeing on some issues. Yet for some Armenian groups, the process of coopertion begins by an assumption of identity of interests and ends with the subservience of Armenia to what they perceive as Russia's interests and desires. The mental structures of primitive ideologues would not allow a government or the people of Armenia to first determine Armenia's interests and then compare these interests with those of other states and thereby pursue whatever that logic requires.

Armenian Communists and some others began by assigning a role and a mission to Russia, by defining its interests whence they extrapolated their own. Russia is what they imagine or wish it to be: nationalistic and imperialistic, a Russia that is anti-Turkish and anti-Turkic by definition and would prefer Armenians over Turks and Azerbaijanis, Christians over Muslims. This visualization has nothing to do with who was governing Russia. If it was Yeltsin, whose government did not fit this image, then Yeltsin did not represent the "real Russia."

Real Russia is there somewhere, hidden in the hallways of the Duma, hidden behind the vague words of Gennady Zhukanov, the leader of Russia's Communist Party, and of Vladimir Zhirinovsky, the Russian extreme nationalist leader, that only true believers could understand, interpret, and act on. The real Russia is out there and is waiting for Armenians to show their loyalty; it would deliver once that loyalty was demonstrated by the genuine believers. And if the present levels of cooperation and strategic calculations were not eliciting the appropriate response, this was only because the cooperation was not sufficient, not systematic— in one word, not wholesome. In this vision, Russia was cast in the role of the insecure lover who constantly needed reinforcement, and each time stronger devotion, so it would at some point respond.

The significance of Azerbaijan for Russia and its peaceful relations with Turkey since World War I will not change by showing more "love and devotion." Russia, including the Russia of Gennady Zhukanov or Vladimir Zhirinovsky, will do nothing more for Armenia than what its national interests allow it to do. Those who believe otherwise are, at best, projecting their own insecurities; at worst, they are solving problems of power in Armenia.

The same argument would apply to those in (but mostly outside) Armenia who would replace Russia with Iran, the United States; or NATO, as the great protector of Armenia. Western intervention in the region has not historically supported Armenian interests, not in deed anyway. They do not do so today. And it is not a matter of not being able to explain Armenian rights and aspirations. It is simply that the United States, the United Kingdom, France, and other nations are capable of determining their own interests.

Whatever respect Russians and Americans may have for Armenia's Christian heritage, whatever love France may have for Armenian culture, whatever sorrow other people may feel for Armenia's "martyrdom," whatever words of sympathy are uttered in various countries toward Armenian aspirations, on issues of significance to them, states act according to their own interests as defined by them and not as projected by Armenians.

The first and most important task for Armenian political parties and leaders is to understand and assess objectively the others' interests, not define these interests based on one's own wishful thinking. Russia is too important a partner to be treated as an insecure lover, needing constant reinforcement and evidence of Armenia's love.

C. The Armenian Revolutionary Federation

Of the "higher missions" under consideration, the one projected by the ARF is the weightiest, most comprehensive, and the most widely known. Its ultimate goal is the establishment of a free country that is independent and unites all historically Armenian territories. Founded in 1890 for the purpose of bringing about reforms in Ottoman Armenia, the ARF adopted independence as a goal in 1919. The First Republic, founded largely through the efforts of the ARF and governed by it, was a year old when the slogan "Free, Independent, and United Armenia" was adopted as the ideal of the party. In a Diasporan setting, where the vision was exiled along with the party, that slogan represented the rectification of all historical injustices, the reward for all martyrdom in the past, the justification for all present sacrifices. It is this Armenia that would offer the promised afterlife for Diasporans who will return and live their dreams.

The strategy to achieve this ideal has evolved over time, and priorities have changed. Yet quite apart from the intricacies of the changes, the quest for the ideal homeland has been known as "Hay Tad," or the Armenian Cause. Even though this term is used by other parties, nonparty groups, and individuals, the ARF considers itself as the guardian of the cause.

Unification did not always have priority in ARF strategy. When in 1920 the ARF lost control of Armenia (which eventually became a constituent republic of the USSR), it was independence that mattered. During the Cold War, the ARF's priority was to see a free and independent Armenia; getting rid of Russian/Communist rule mattered most. For that, the ARF cooperated with the enemies of the USSR, including the United States and Turkey. Since the 1970s, unification of historic Armenian territories, inevitably to Soviet Armenia, had taken precedence over the other dimensions of the ideal.

This shift had its logic. The "united" was alleged to be more attainable than the "free" or "independent." The liberation of the Turkish occupied lands would come with the help of the Soviet Union, an enemy of Turkey and a super power of which Armenia was a constituent element.

Neither independence nor the Karabagh problem was on the immediate agenda of the ARF when Karabagh erupted in 1988 and Armenia undertook steps to achieve secession from the USSR beginning in 1989. Both events were considered inconsistent with ARF's policy of improving relations with and reliance on the USSR. These events confounded the ARF, which opposed both struggles at first. With the dissolution of the USSR, the ARF needed to make adjustments in its strategy and rhetoric. The party developed a deep, well cultivated, and lasting aversion, to put it mildly, toward the movement responsible for the disruption that ARF strategy had been caused, for the ANM, and for its leader, Levon Ter-Petrossian, from the day the Karabagh Committee was formed.

Nowadays, the ARF defines the Armenian Cause as "One Nation, One Homeland." In the context of this Cause, the nation has three components: Armenians in Armenia, Armenians in Karabagh, and Armenians in the Diaspora. The homeland has many more: Armenia, Karabagh, Javakhk (in the Republic of Georgia, Armenia's northern neighbor), Nakhichevan (a noncontiguous part of Azerbaijan to the southwest of Armenia), and historic Western Armenia or eastern Turkey, to the west of the republic of Armenia.

Within this perspective, Armenia is only one component, which happens to have advanced further in the process than the others: It is recognized as a state by the international community. Next comes Karabagh, which is liberated and has declared independence, but has not yet been recognized internationally as an independent state or as part of Armenia. Then comes Javakhk, according to ARF strategists, the Armenian population that has just started to assert its rights. The unification of the others will necessarily follow.

This dream of remaking the Armenian world, a dream that would also remake three of Armenia's four neighbors, is the master plan of the ARF, which is also the plan's strategist and executor. Armenia is only one of the pieces, its government only one of the levers of power, and its people only one of the armies assigned to fight the wars, albeit the one to carry the heaviest burden of fighting and dying.

From the ARF perspective, the new state of Armenia has neither the vision nor the resources to bring about the resolution of the Armenian Cause, unless, possibly, if it were governed by the ARF, in which case it could assume responsibility for a larger share of the project. Ter-Petrossian's Armenia, with its call for "normalcy" and all that "normally" implied in foreign policy matters, was even less qualified to pursue this dream. That Ter-Petrossian's Armenia would reject the recognition of the Genocide as the basis for the country's foreign policy and would seek to normalize relations with Turkey was sufficient to characterize him, his administration, and the ANM as antinational. In fact, the ARF depicted Ter-Petrossian and his associates as the worst enemy of the national project and, therefore, of the Armenian nation.

Finally, for the ARF, a national project of such magnitude, a vision as grand as the Armenian Cause, can be carried out only by an historically and morally validated authority, designated democratically or otherwise. The political program of nation-building is formulated and structured in a manner that makes the ARF, by definition, the only qualified organization that can pursue it, define its stages, or determine its strategy. Within the larger scheme, Armenia and Karabagh, independence and unification constitute what could be used or sacrificed in the name of the higher ideal.

By raising the national project to the level of a dream so grand and so distant, the ARF's vision, strategy, and judgment have acquired a degree of immunity against criticism and verification. Just as it is difficult to know whether one is moving toward hell or heaven while alive, it is difficult to subject ARF policies to the normal methods of verification in order to determine whether the ARF has been able to bring Armenians closer to the realization of the ideal. The ARF can always find some lofty goal or principle with which to critique and degrade anyone else's policies, justify its own changes, and label any criticism toward it as antinational behavio or worse.

The ARF believes that the combination of age, heroes, and grandeur of vision bestows on it exclusively the right to define and strategize Armenian interests and to represent the Armenian people in all places, at all times, under all circumstances, with or without votes, because the party considers itself the microcosm of the nation.

NORMALCY VERSUS NATIONAL IDEOLOGY

The last three groups described above share a number of characteristics.

The first is their proclivity to assess events, facts, and choices in terms of a predetermined and set view of the world. All three seem to seek certainty, coherence, and predictability in a region that has little or none of these; all three seek to find them in ideological constructs. Decisions would not be made on the basis of their intrinsic benefit or harm to Armenia but on the degree to which they preserve the coherence of its worldview. In fact, available options would not be considered, if precluded by the assumptions of the worldview.

All three groups attempt to gain a moral high ground by characterizing their worldviews as "national ideologies." The word *national* is expected to bestow on these constructs an a priori sanctity, a quasi-religious sanction; and the word *ideology* ought to endow them with a sense of universality, coherence, and rationality as well as to give it the appearance of scientific foundation.

The term *national* must also be understood as the opposite of *individual*. The promotion of a "national" ideology is an attempt by political parties to intimidate citizens not to think of politics as an expression of their own self-interest but to accept it as the destiny of the collective. Individual self-interest and national interest end up as opposites, close to being mutually exclusive, rather than constituting a continuum. National interest, defined abstractly by one person or group, determines what the citizens' self-interest should be.

The difference between the ANM and the other groups resided exactly in this point. The ANM, however inadequately, recognized and accepted the "national" to mean the sum total of the personal self-interest of citizens. The other groups, through their ideological offerings, ascribed the "national" a different basis of legitimacy and a different origin than the parts of the nation. For Vazgen Manukian's NDU, failure to agree with his national ideology signaled a lack of character and strength and a moral failure. For the ARF, rejecting its ideals and strategies is a sure sign of being a "bad Armenian." For the communistic groups, disagreeing with their vision constituted evidence of being a suspect person.

The issue is not whether one has a vision for one's country. Political parties and leaders do often have visions, usually called programs, that may be based on ideals they share with fellow citizens and hope to engage the citizenry in their realization. But a program or vision with ideals is different from ideologically inspired worldviews. Ideologies divide nations and groups into the good and the bad; they detach and alienate, even dehumanize, segments of a people. Ideologies, whether fascist, nationalist, communist, or other, provide self-righteous and self-centered people with the moral and political justification to compel individuals to behave and think in a certain way, to resist the temptation of reasoning for and by themselves and determining what is best for them and for the nation. The promotion of national ideologies constitutes an attempt to impose definitions and identities.

Ideologies are higher than laws, particularly when they are branded "national ideologies." They can justify the use of violence to achieve power and the use of power to compel citizens to be and to behave in a manner that proves the ideology right.

If the ANM and the Ter-Petrossian-led administrations can be faulted for violation of the electoral law, then ideological parties are prone to violate the whole constitutional order. For the Communists, it is an external force that will bring them to power; the Red Army did it in 1920; they may be hoping it will happen again. The NDU has the "people" freed of any constraints. The ARF has its paramilitary groups, possibly needed in a country such as Lebanon, but illegal elsewhere, including Armenia. If Ter-Petrossian recognized irregularities and considered them wrong, the ideologists have yet to denounce their earlier claims of a right to the violent overthrow of government in the name of a higher goal, and their actual use of that right. In fact, they have reiterated it.

One paradox worth thinking about is that parties and leaders who rejected the use of violence against the Soviets as a means to achieve independence and democracy asserted that right as a matter of principle against the ANM and Ter-Petrossian. To declare, as these parties did, that the Ter-Petrossian administration was worse than the Soviet regime or even the worst ever in Armenian history is, of course, street rhetoric and cannot be taken seriously. This apparent paradox says something about these parties and their leaders, about their priorities and self-images rather than about Ter-Petrossian or his administration.

For the ARF and Communists especially, another dimension of the word *national*, as opposed to a-national, is its evocation of Turkey. Especially for the CPA, DPA, and the ARF, politics is national if it is based on anti-Turkism. A politics becomes an ideology when anti-Turkism dominates one's politics. The Communists and the ARF especially assign a central roles to the questions of Armenia's relation with Turkey and of the Genocide in Armenia's foreign policy. Vazgen Manukian has been less enthusiastic than the others on this issue, although as a presidential candidate who received the support of the Communists and ARF in 1996 he, too, made the "Armenian Cause" part of his campaign platform.

For Ter-Petrossian, the establishment of diplomatic relations with Turkey without any preconditions was a logical corollary to the basic principle of Armenia's foreign policy of normalizing relations with all neighbors. Turkey's recognition of the Armenian Genocide was not a precondition for the development of normal relations. He considered the Genocide a historical and moral, not a political, issue. The Genocide was a catastrophic event in the history of the Armenian people that had to be documented; its causes, processes, and consequences analyzed and understood; its victims remembered in dignity; its lessons drawn for humanity; and its barbarity and inhumanity exposed. The Genocide was not a worldview or a philosophy; it was not a principle, especially one on which Armenia's foreign policy could be based.

The ANM view, most clearly articulated by Ter-Petrossian, represented a shift in Armenian political thinking whose importance cannot be underestimated. Conventional wisdom asserted that Turkey was the eternal enemy, ever waiting for a chance to repeat 1915. In addition, the losses from the Genocide justified Armenian territorial demands from Turkey. Normalization of relations was anathema. This view of the place of Turkey in Armenian thinking was widely accepted before independence, promoted by Soviet ideology, supported by the Communist Party, and enhanced by the processing of the Genocide experience in the Diaspora. The ANM position negated acquired conventional political wisdom, challenged the collective memory, and threatened to make irrelevant much of the politicized discourse around the Genocide in Armenia and the Diaspora.

But for their opponents, especially the Communists and the ARF, this policy was antinational, if not worse. Being anti-Turkish, a reflexive reaction to history, had been transformed into an article of faith and elevated to the level of a principle of strategy. One could determine what was good for Armenia and Armenians by seeing if it was bad for Turkey. Any strategy built on this belief sounded not only emotionally satisfying but also strategically unassailable.

If Turkey was bad and genocidal by definition, then Armenians, by definition, had nowhere to go but to Russia and, to some extent, Iran for protection. Survival being more important than anything else, a pro-Soviet and pro-Russian position becomes as much a guide to foreign policy and security concepts as does being anti-Turkish.

This is the point at which the circumstances of Ter-Petrossian's resignation, the traditional Armeno-Turkish antagonism, and the debate on Karabagh intersect. Turkish-Armenian relations were injected into the Karabagh debate in a number of ways, the most immediate being the Turkish blockade of Armenia in support of Azerbaijan.

The border between Turkey and Armenia was closed during the Soviet period, except for the weekly passenger train that crossed it from Gumri (then Leninakan), near the border, into Turkey. Following the independence of Armenia, which Turkey recognized, the two countries engaged in negotiations for the establishment of diplomatic relations, on the basis of which border crossings could be regulated. Given the history of Armeno-Turkish relations, the establishment of diplomatic relations was not expected to be easy. But it was altogether possible and with in reach.

In 1992, when the railroad from Georgia that normally carried wheat imports into Armenia was disrupted because of the Abkhazian conflict, Turkey permitted European donated wheat to reach Armenia using Turkish ports and Turkish rail, in light of the progress made in bilateral negotiations. The cooperation continued through the winter of 1992 and 1993 until Armenian forces occupied Kelbajar in the spring of 1993, at which time Turkey interrupted those shipments in solidarity with Azerbaijan. For all practical purposes, the border was closed again. Since then Turkey has linked the opening of the border and the normalization of relations with Armenia to the resolution or progress in the solution of the Karabagh conflict.

By acting in support of Azerbaijan while also a member of the OSCE Minsk Group, many people came to see Turkey see as part of the problem rather than part of the solution. It did not require a leap of imagination for the traditional anti-Turkish strategists to bring the historical antagonism into play in the debate on the Karabagh problem, particularly when keeping the border closed served Azerbaijan's strategy of strangling the Armenian economy and forcing concessions that Armenia was not ready to make and never did make.

But the impact of this factor went far beyond views of history and neighborliness. To the extent that the Turkish border included rail and road communications of strategic significance, especially for Armenia's access to export markets, the opening of the Turkish border was an integral component of the argument on whether Armenia could develop economically without resolving the Karabagh problem. And that was, as seen earlier, the fundamental difference between Ter-Petrossian and Kocharian. However, if for Kocharian the argument was one of practical calculations, for the Communists and the ARF the border issue had much deeper implications. The opening of the border would entail normalization of relations with Turkey, which would gradually reduce the perception of Turkey as a security threat and thus would lessen Armenia's economic and security dependence on other nations. Thus, the problem of Karabagh was linked to the question of independence, the possibility of effectuating a basic change in Armenia's security concept, and achieving normalcy.

One also has to imagine what such changes, had they been successful, would have meant for the conventional opposition, especially for the Communists and the ARF. For them, Ter-Petrossian was undermining every pillar of their thinking about the past and about the future about their identities and their role in both.

Genocide and anti-Turkism had become so integral to the identity of these parties and their followers, to their sense of a wronged history, to their need for justice now, and to their vision of a redeeming future that it was not difficult to identify those who called for normalcy as the devils personified. Thus, it became possible to transform opposition to a political program into personal hatred and vilification of Ter-Petrossian and of the individuals around him who shared his worldview. Normalcy was a dangerous notion that had to be neutralized, along with its carriers.

The personalization of the ideological opposition is significant in two ways. First, for some parties that shun rational debate on goals, strategies, and tactics, personalized hatred works better than political argumentation and discourse on choices. Where there are villains, there must also be good guys; where there are traitors, there will be patriots.

Second, the leaders of an emerging third force believed the rhetoric of the opposition parties who had designated Ter-Petrossian and a few around him as the villains. Kocharian and Vazgen Sargsian believed that by compelling Ter-Petrossian's resignation, they were removing the major if not the only obstacle to internal unity and to unity between Armenia and the Diaspora; both unities were necessary if their alternative solution was to work.

THE "PARTY OF KARABAGH"

As strange as it might seem, the best way to understand Karabagh is to look at it as a party. In a manner of speaking, the "Party of Karabagh" is the oldest: It is as old as the problem of Karabagh and of Karabagh itself. It is also the simplest. The people of Karabagh know what they are against: They do not wish to be dominated by Azerbaijan or by Azerbaijanis. Under the Azerbaijanis, whom Karabagh Armenians refer as "Turks," Karabagh was treated as a colony in the classical sense of the word, with all the economic and social underdevelopment that term evokes. Karabagh Armenians cannot accept Azerbaijani rule especially now, after having been blockaded, bombed, deported, and altogether alienated by Azerbaijan since 1990.

The people of Karabagh also know what they would like: Their goal is to rid themselves of Azerbaijani domination. Whether that goal is achieved through union with Armenia, independence or, as proposed by some people, through integration with Russia, is secondary. As the name implies, this is a single-issue party. The issue is Karabagh. All else is secondary and means little: Relations with Turkey, democracy, economic system, or governmental structure mean little. Karabagh Armenians have little use for ideological programs and complex political arguments. They have deep-rooted beliefs and biases, that reflect their geography, social structure, and what they believe their history has been; these biases cannot easily be dislodged, even with the most complex arguments.

Karabagh Armenians, as other people in their situation in history and around the world today, have their own way of learning and processing history. Karabagh Armenians also have their own way of digesting what they have learned and of integrating it with what they already know. Alien ideologies have difficulty surviving in Karabagh unless they adapt themselves to these mental structures supported by social institutions that are more important than political ones. Differences between Karabagh Armenians are less significant than differences between different views within one political party elsewhere.

Two sets of circumstances complicate the seemingly simple political agenda of Karabagh: Is there a strategy to achieve that goal? And, who speaks for the people of Karabagh (or, how does a people become a party)?

Karabagh is primarily a "foreign policy" issue. It is a problem not because Armenia or Armenians do not know what they would like to do with it, but because another country, Azerbaijan, has its own plans for it. Whether as a constituent republic of the USSR contesting Karabagh's demand for unification with Armenia, or as an independent republic insisting on territorial integrity, Azerbaijan is the antagonist, and Azerbaijan is unwilling to let go of Karabagh. In that, Azerbaijan has the support of the international community. In addition, Armenia is involved as the defender of Karabagh, and the Armenian Diaspora joined in very early in support of Karabagh.

Moreover, Moscow, too, was involved, first as the arbiter of the dispute in its capacity as the Soviet capital, second as the main party supplying arms to both sides, and third as the neighboring country with the most influence on the parties to the conflict. Finally, other neighbors, the OSCE, and the international community became involved as the conflict was militarized, the post–Cold War international games began, and oil and pipeline politics kicked in.

A local political conflict quickly turned brutal and was soon militarized, nationalized, regionalized, and internationalized. To what extent have these transformations helped or hurt the cause of Karabagh and in what ways has the substance of the conflict itself changed through these transformations are the subjects of another study. Nonetheless, three conclusions can be drawn. First, the issue has been vested with economic, partisan, political, and geostrategic interests by sides directly and indirectly involved in the conflict. Second, neither war nor diplomacy has so far compelled a solution acceptable to all concerned. Third, the Party of Karabagh cannot yet find its way out of the morass.

The second set of components complicating the work of the Karabagh Party is the question of leadership: Who speaks for this party?

In a society of tightly knit structures, reinforced by the economic and military exigencies, governmental and military leaders of Karabagh have had ultimate responsibility in this matter of representation. That is why the ANM, even in its heyday and at the time of the closest cooperation with the Karabagh leadership, did not create branches in Karabagh. The two political parties that are registered and have branches in Karabagh, the Communists and the ARF, do not represent alternative programs.

Since 1992, the leadership of Karabagh has consisted of a few strong-willed and talented personalities. The most important was Robert Kocharian. Others include Serge Sargsian—subsequently a member of the Cabinet of Armenia; Leonard Petrossian, Prime Minister of Karabagh under Kocharian; Samvel Babayan, who rose from the ranks of the fighters to become Commander of the Karabagh Army and now Defense Minister with much control over the economic and political processes as well as foreign policy; and Arkadi Ghukasian, who first served as Minister of Foreign Affairs and replaced Kocharian as President of Karabagh. Whether elected or appointed, these officials have governed Karabagh more in the style of the elders of a large family or, to continue with the basic analogy, as the powerful leaders of a political party.

For most of the duration of the Ter-Petrossian administration, the governments of Karabagh and Armenia worked together basically through regular, continuing, and often intense consultations. The assumptions underlying these consultations were that the interests of Armenia and Karabagh are essentially the same and that divergences were similar to differences within a family and could be managed.

There were, of course divergences, often strong disagreements, but until September 1997 they remained, for the most part, private. Opposition parties argued publicly and often with passion about the Karabagh problem, but the parties as well as their argument remained largely irrelevant to the negotiations.

Two important developments changed that relationship. First, the position of the leaders of the Karabagh Party regarding a compromise based solution changed. Some argued about the terms of the proposed agreement; others were not sure that the compromises were necessary at this time. Still others, essentially the defense ministers, had doubts regarding the return of those territories that had been occupied for security and strategic reasons during the war. On more than one occasion, Vazgen Sargsian has argued publicly that land won by blood cannot be returned, bringing his position closer to those who believed that the Karabagh problem was a question of rectifying history, although he did not always think so.

The second development was the rise in Armenia of a Party of Karabagh, in the form of the Yerkrapahs. Originally an organization of veterans of the war, the organization enjoyed Defense Minister Vazgen Sargsian's support. In 1995 eight Yerkrapahs were elected to the National Assembly with the endorsement of the ANM and without a particular political program of their own: They supported Ter-Petrossian, while watchful of the interests of veterans in the Parliament.

As the internal struggle in administration circles intensified, the Yerkrapahs were metamorphosed into a political party. As Kocharian and the two ministers decided to challenge Ter-Petrossian, wavering ANM and pro-Ter-Petrossian deputies were directed to the Yerkrapah group in Parliament as the core of the new opposition. Enough deputies changed sides to bring about a loss of majority for Ter-Petrossian and, ultimately, his resignation.

Since then, the Yerkrapahs, lacking a political program, have joined up with the small right-wing and somewhat militant Republican Party to change their image and role and to become a political party and win elections. The Yerkrapahs are very much part of the Karabagh party, and until recently they reflected a single issue image, aligned in general with the Karabagh leadership.

In most matters, the Party of Karabagh, whether in Karabagh or Armenia, is nonideological. Karabagh is at the top of the hierarchy of concerns; all else is subject to its logic. The leaders of the Karabagh party themselves, Kocharian, Babayan, Vazgen Sargsian, and Serge Sargsian, are essentially pragmatic people and will go with what works in the economic and political arenas. All four, especially the current defense ministers, consider that the emphasis on the Genocide instills the wrong values in the new generation. The psychology of the victim runs contrary to the self-image and spirit they believe must be encouraged in a nation that has won the war. They see relations with Turkey from a pragmatic point of view. If they serve that purpose, and in the ministers' view they do, then normalization with Turkey is a goal to be pursued and achieved, although not at the expense of any concessions on Karabagh.

Within the larger categories of the Armenian political spectrum discussed earlier, the Party of Karabagh stands in the middle. Being devoid of ideological content, it is closer to the ANM and Ter-Petrossian, with whom they were able to work for so long and through so many difficulties. In order to have a credible candidacy and a reasonable chance of solving at least some problems, Prime Minister Kocharian, later Acting President Kocharian, put together a coalition of the Yerkrapahs, and a few other parties, including the ARF. He also made gestures to the latter, including legalizing their party, releasing party leaders (but not rank and file members) charged with criminal activities by the previous administration. Kocharian has also made gestures toward the Diaspora, such as raising the issue of Genocide recognition with Turkey and at the UN.

The Party of Karabagh can retain its purity and clarity of direction as long as it is a single-issue party. Once a political party in Armenia, it must assume responsibility not only for the solution of the Karabagh problem but also for the administration of all governmental affairs, the budget, and other issues, such as the rate of unemployment, inflation, budget deficits, education, salaries of teachers, and pensions—all this while the government services substantial and expensive armed forces and an arms race with Azerbaijan.

These actions are discussed in some detail in subsequent chapters. But Kocharian's declared foreign policy principles have not deviated substantially from those of the previous administration. While raised as a subject of discussion, Genocide recognition was not made a precondition for the establishment of diplomatic relations with Turkey, and Armenia has not presented Turkey with any territorial demands. The principle of a balanced foreign policy also seems to have been preserved through Armenia's continuing cooperation with the OSCE mediating team, and relations with European institutions and the United States do not seem to have been affected during the first year.

Kocharian began his presidency with a major handicap but also with a number of assumptions. Being a hero and leader of Karabagh did not secure him a political support base in Armenia. By leading the challenge to Ter-Petrossian, Kocharian became the de facto leader of the Party of Karabagh. Curiously, although as President he controls the administration of Armenia, Kocharian has no direct control over the two components of his party: Karabagh, which he once governed but which came under the control of those leaders who remained behind, primarily defense minister Samvel Babayan; and the Yerkrapahs, whose loyalty is to Vazgen Sargsian.

Kocharian believed that, having removed Ter-Petrossian, he could create unity—that elusive cure—within and unity without, that parties would transcend their differences and work for the common good, for the simple program of building the country, making it strong economically and keeping it strong militarily. A strong Armenia would compel Azerbaijan to accept the most concessions, while the Armenian side would make as few concessions, as late as possible. He believed that he could borrow some of the weapons that the conventional opposition parties had in their arsenal as a means to get them and the Diaspora on board.

Of course, his hope for success depended also on a number of measures to be implemented on the domestic scene, including more discipline in government and more efficiency in the administration and bureaucracy, a comprehensive and effective campaign against corruption, and a more friendly business and foreign investment environment.

In substance Kocharian's program relied first on the spirit of unity he hoped he could create around the national cause, Karabagh, by a more inclusive relationship with the opposition. Second, he hoped for a more productive relationship with the Diaspora, which he considered the ensurer of foreign aid and investments, even if that required that he pay more attention to the one issue that seemed to touch Diasporans deeply—the recognition of the Genocide. Kocharian hoped he could build bridges over time and space.

4.

Bridges Over Time and Space

One can understand so much about the politics of a leader and his party by identifying what they do with the past and what role they assign to history—regardless of any particular interpretation of it. It is possible to argue, for example, that post-Soviet Armenian communists are trying to justify the past; that the Armenian Revolutionary Federation (ARF) is attempting to glorify it, hoping for its repetition; that Vazgen Manukian is trying to transform it into an energizing principle of power and legitimacy; that Vazgen Sargsian wants to avenge the past; and that Ter-Petrossian and the Armenian National Movement (ANM) struggled to transcend it.

Kocharian wishes to ignore the past. He believes the past is only a burden, an obstacle to clear thinking. He approached his task as a "reconstructionist." The way the various components making up the present had been assembled in Armenia and the region did not seem to work, he thought. Kocharian wants to see if the same components can be reassembled differently, in a manner that would produce a very different and particular result. Components are assigned a function that sets aside their previous role and their subjective and ideological identity. Each component would perform according to the new design, if it understood the project and acted accordingly or was coaxed to do so.

Political parties represent one set of components, just as Armenia, Karabagh, and the Diaspora each constitute another. The underpinning of Kocharian's call for unity was his expectation that parties and leaders would see the simplicity and wisdom of the national project and, since each of them claimed to be dedicated to it, they would respond and work together. Disagreements and conflicts between the various elements would be managed better than before, and that is what was required: Better management of existing resources. Kocharian's world is an essentially nonpolitical, if not antipolitical world, in fact, an engineer's world. Unity, for him, rested on mathematical calculations of the capabilities and potential of each component rather than on the politics of overcoming conflicts of principles, personalities, programs, or policies.

THE ELUSIVE POLITICS OF UNITY

Few words have been used more often in Armenian political debates than the word *unity*. In the minds of many people, the idea of unity is the panacea to all ills; it is the slogan for those who want to project the highest ideals and noblest intentions.

Calls for unity have a curious history. They tend to come from people who started off by "disuniting." Armenians in the Ottoman Empire, for example, were united under the Church, when political parties emerged, disuniting themselves from the traditional national structure. Once they separated themselves from the existing structure, they then called for unity. Vazgen Manukian and his associates "disunited" from the ANM, founded the National Democratic Union (NDU), and then called for national unity. Kocharian and his group first disunited themselves from Ter-Petrossian, then called for unity. In fact, every time a group of individuals register as a political party at the Ministry of Justice, they are technically committing an act of "disunion." They are stating that they are different and separate; they are instituting a line of demarcation. At the end, most put out calls for unity of some kind or another.

Yet I cannot remember many cases in which an organization, institution, or party has given up its autonomy, structures, goals, budget, or controls in the name of unity, whether in Armenia or in the Diaspora.

Unity can refer to four levels: Political unity within Armenia; unity of action and diplomacy between Armenia and Karabagh;

agreement around national ideals and strategies within the Diaspora, Armenia, and Karabagh; and unity within Diaspora communities.

Unity within Armenia

Unity within Armenia is the easiest to imagine, but it has still been difficult to achieve. Agreement on a Constitution (determining the rules of the game, including how to resolve differences) represents one kind of unity. That is the legal, the highest kind of unity. There is no question where the center of gravity is located: the state and the head of state.

In time of a crisis, such as war or similar national emergency, a nation could also achieve political unity by setting aside differences and focusing on the resolution of the crisis.

This did not happen during the 1992 to 1994 war with Azerbaijan. The disunity had nothing to do with elections. There was no question of the result of the 1991 elections; the Constitution, the ratification of which was questioned in 1995, had not yet been submitted to a referendum; the country was being governed by laws passed by the first Parliament, of which just about every opposition leader was a member.

Ter-Petrossian did not turn unity into a political aim or slogan. He accepted the opposition and noncooperation of opposition parties, even in times of war, as long as it was nonviolent. Yet he attempted to practice unity. He invited his main rival, Vazgen Manukian, to serve as Defense Minister in his first administration. He appointed Paruyr Hayrikian as administrator of the Lachin district. They both served and then resigned. In 1992, Ter-Petrossian invited all party leaders, including the ARF, to become members of Armenia's national Security Council, where debate on the critical issues took place. Most opposition parties, including the NDU, ARF, and Communist parties, refused the offer. Ter-Petrossian had a number of Karabagh leaders and Diasporan Armenians serving in high offices in his administration. The number of individuals who accepted the invitation is fewer than those who were invited to contribute to state building. Ter-Petrossian initiated and strongly supported the All-Armenian

Fund, the first and only institution that brings together the leaders of Armenia and Karabagh, as well as representatives of all major organizations and prominent individuals of the Diaspora. He also did not hesitate to strike back (with words and deeds) at groups, domestic or Diasporan, that threatened the stability and tranquillity of the country. For these actions and for reasons discussed earlier, Ter-Petrossian was presented as a divisive figure.

Kocharian believed he could succeed where Ter-Petrossian had failed. He believed Ter-Petrossian had not tried hard enough and had alienated opposition parties in Armenia and that by banning the dominant political party from the Diaspora, the ARF, he had alienated the Diaspora in general.

Kocharian has acted to rebuild the bridges. One of his first acts as Acting President was to lift the ban against the ARF. He invited the leaders of parties formerly opposing the Ter-Petrossian administration to serve as his advisers. Three accepted: Paruyr Hayrikian of the National Self-Determination Union (NSDU), Vahan Hovannisian of the ARF, and Aram Sargsian of the Democratic Party of Armenia (DPA). Vazgen Manukian permitted his deputy, Davit Vardanian, to serve in the presidential administration.

Kocharian has also created a presidential council in which all political parties are represented, and he has given ministerial posts to members of different parties, although ministries dealing with economic affairs are headed by professionals and the power ministries are led by his associates, Vazgen Sargsian and Serge Sargsian. He has also opened up to the Diaspora in a number of ways. The Minister of Foreign Affairs and one advisor are Diaspora-born. He has a more public-relations-oriented approach to Diaspora contacts. Kocharian has also announced a major conference on Diaspora-Armenia relations to take place in September 1999, in Yerevan.

Whether sharing positions with other parties is sufficient to produce unity in Armenia is not clear. Party leaders (past and potential presidential candidates) acting as advisers to the President have publicly disagreed with Kocharian; one even signed a petition circulating in the National Assembly in October 1998 calling for the President's impeachment. The ARF, whose leader is one of the presidential advisers, has organized rallies against the President's domestic policies, trying to distance itself from the administration. Karen Demirjian and other influential politicians, such as Davit Shahnazarian, have refused to have anything to do with the administration.

It seems as though it is politics as usual in Yerevan. Lacking his own power base, Kocharian must rely on the Yerkrapah majority to pass legislation in Parliament, and on the ARF and the DPA for political support outside Parliament and in the Diaspora. Neither Communists nor the ARF has given that support without a price. They have expected Kocharian to come closer to the ideological tenets of their programs, especially in foreign policy.

Kocharian's eclecticism has invited each party supporting him to demand more loyalty from him. Lacking an ideological zeal of their own, Kocharian and the other leaders of the Party of Karabagh can accommodate the ideologists up to a point. But in this exchange, it seems that Kocharian is giving more than he is receiving. The aura of unity and cooperation has been bought at the expense of being constantly challenged to prove his loyalty alternately to the Yerkrapahs, the ARF, and the Communists. These parties have ceded little and expect increasingly more. They will go to great lengths to use their position within the Kocharian administration to consolidate their political base and increase their power, waiting for the day when they will replace Kocharian, by whatever means, and implement their full program rather than the symbolic pieces that Kocharian is borrowing from each to create the aura of a consensus.

One issue on which opposition parties had agreed during the Ter-Petrossian administration was the need to give Parliament more powers, taking them away from the president. Kocharian agreed with the opposition and promised a constitutional amendment on the transfer of some presidential powers to Parliament when elected. Once elected, however, he must not have thought the Constitution really gave much power to the president, and he has opposed any substantial changes in the balance of power. One can safely presume the same change of heart would have visited any candidates who had been elected president.

Armenia and Karabagh

Relations between Armenia and Karabagh should be the most organic. For the most part, the two entities worked closely through discussion and consensus. Yet, Karabagh "disunited" gradually from Armenia, until it tipped the balance against Armenia's president. The new de facto leader of Karabagh, Samvel Babayan, has also been "disuniting" himself from the new president of Armenia, the former leader of Karabagh, accusing Yerevan of not having a "clear stance" on the compromises Yerevan is ready to make.

There are three problems in the Armenia-Karabagh relationship. Armenia has responsibilities toward international law and the international community that Karabagh, not recognized by any other government as a sovereign state, does not. Karabagh can afford to be a single-agenda party; Armenia cannot, whoever its president. At the end, Armenia and its government, rather than the leaders of Karabagh, will be held responsible for whatever happens to Karabagh by the international community and by history.

Nonetheless, there are organic links that have created a common area of operations. The interests of the two entities must compel them to work together. Karabagh can define its interests as being independent of Armenia's interests, needs, and resources only by risking more than it can afford to.

Unity of the Armenian World

Unity of the Armenian world—Armenia, Karabagh, and the Diaspora or the diasporas—is of a different order. This unity constitutes the ultimate challenge to the ideas of abstracted nationalism and national identity.

Although the time of illusions and misplaced expectations is gone, the assumptions underlying Kocharian's hopes have yet to be fully tested: that the Diaspora can be organized up to its potential, that those who speak for it in fact can marshal all of the Diaspora's resources for the national agenda as defined by a president of Armenia, and that the Diaspora's potential will make a significant change in Armenia's fortunes.

One charge against Ter-Petrossian's perceived antagonism toward the Diaspora consisted of the "milking cow" argument: that Armenia's government looked at the Diaspora strictly as a source of cash and did not want any of its participation or advice. The best evidence, it was argued, is the 1995 Constitution, which prohibits dual citizenship, depriving Diaspora Armenians of a natural right to receive Armenian citizenship and feel part of the homeland. The Ter-Petrossian administration had resolved that problem by creating a special passport that Diaspora Armenians could receive while still citizens of other countries. The passport gave them all rights and privileges of a citizen, except the rights to vote and to be elected to office and the duty to serve in the armed forces.

Dual citizenship is a complicated issue that must accommodate a number of sensitive factors. Kocharian campaigned in favor of a constitutional amendment on that subject as part of his policy of improving relations with the Diaspora. Yet a number of political groups in Armenia oppose it, including Vazgen Sargsian and the Yerkrapahs. No further effort has been made to change the Constitution in this, either.

Unity within the Diaspora

Diaspora structures are discussed in the next chapter; here, however, one phenomenon needs to be pointed out in the context of unity.

Calls for unity have been abundant in the Diaspora: Church unity, party unity, community unity. But institutions and organizations, once disunited, have not reunited, even when the reason for their disunity has disappeared. Each organization, large or small, feels that something of the Armenian will die if it dissolves itself, even if it is no longer relevant or useful. Maybe it is the law of inertia or the inability of some people to live with the loss of power and control. It may be the sense of self-preservation at its extreme.

The Diaspora finds it more natural to find common ground on the past rather than the future. Most Diaspora Armenians will continue to imagine their future as part of countries in which they are settled, and not in Armenia or Karabagh, calls by national ideologists to "return home" notwithstanding. Diasporan organizations have too much invested in current structures, in too many ways, for them now to give up their structures, hierarchies, and zones of influence. Change may still occur in the future.

UNITY AND THE PROBLEM OF LEGITIMACY

Unity as a political program raises the question of the legitimacy of power. Under the best of circumstances, "disunions" occur as a result of substantial differences on fundamental issues of national interest and on the direction of the future. The Armenian world is facing many such issues. It is quite natural that there would be substantial differences on social, economic, and other issues, as well as on Karabagh, relations with neighbors, and other foreign policy concerns in Armenia. Yet there is general agreement on the major issues that must be resolved in the social and economic arenas. Differences exist on priorities, on causal relationships between issues, and on who can better resolve these issues. Some agenda items in Armenia are closer to the hearts of Diasporans than are others.

Whatever the reasons for the fragmentation of the past, bringing about unity today—of agendas, goals, efforts, or of organizations—raises some questions: unity around what idea, goal or priority? around which institution, organization, or leader?

Disunity is legitimate and even necessary in a country or community. It is the expression of the right to formulate and articulate differing views and programs and to pursue differing solutions. In some cases, appeals for unity aim at eliminating useless and petty quarrels between personalities, or at setting aside secondary issues in an effort to resolve a national crisis. In other cases, a call for unity is a call to suppress alternative views and new agendas and to neutralize opponents. A party making the appeal for unity expects the other parties to unite behind its agenda, its worldview and, of course, its leadership; otherwise it could dissolve itself as a party and unite with another—just as a leader could remove himself from the political scene. In that situation, unity becomes a euphemism for dictatorship, an attempt to achieve through sloganeering and demagogic appeals what could not be achieved otherwise. At such times, one issue is considered larger than "politics as usual" or times are considered "unusual" or "critical." In these instances, appeals for unity constitute calls to bypass the functioning framework—either by transcending it or by trampling on it, usually both.

This is the stuff of which coups d'etats and revolutions are made. It is the de-legitimization of the existing legal framework and the adoption of another principle of legitimacy of power: the power of a person, ideology, or party that is supposed to transcend the common, to reach out to a vision or ideology bigger than what the political system can achieve, to elevate a person in a way that normal political procedures would not. It is the legitimacy of power based on the attributes of an ideology or person or party that transcends the partisan and fragmented spectrum and fractious politics that democracy entails.

"Unity" can become the mechanism through which politics based on the interests of the individual—essential for democracy—is left behind. It is all done in the name of a principle higher than the individual, a principle within which the role of the individual is minimized and the role of the "idea," "vision," or "ideology" is placed above all else, giving the holder of the idea, vision, or ideology power and legitimacy, possibly beyond the law. Unity in these cases is a mechanism to achieve power, a principle to legitimize it, and also an ideology for the exercise of that power.

That is the reason the ANM, leading the democratic opposition to the rule of the Communist Party in Armenia in 1988–1990, did not challenge that party outside the law, however lacking Soviet law was. The ANM wanted the popular will to be legitimized through the legal process, even if it was Soviet law, whether the question was ousting the Communists from power in Armenia or Armenia's secession from the USSR.

That may also be the reason that the main argument of the opposition, partly united in 1996, was that times were not "normal," meaning within the norms, despite what Ter-Petrossian was asserting, and that the country was in "crisis." That is why the opposition's program called for the abolition of the Constitution and for the dissolution of the Parliament under a Manukian presidency. It also called for governing the country by a security council under emergency rule as the "crisis" mandated, on the basis of a "national ideology," a "vision," which in their view Ter-Petrossian and the ANM "lacked,' all in the name of a unity that the ANM and Ter-Petrossian were unable to achieve. This is how it then became natural for the opposition to take to the streets and to resort to violence against the Parliament building and the leaders of the Parliament. Long before the elections, the leaders of the two main parties in the opposition, Manukian for the NDU and Vahan Hovannisian for the ARF, had asserted more than once the rights to use violence and to act beyond the law in the name of a higher principle, a higher ideal.

When international observers found irregularities in the 1995 and 1996 elections in Armenia, Ter-Petrossian and the government recognized that there had been violations of the law. The NDU, the ARF, and others responsible for the violence have not recognized any wrongdoing; in fact, they continue to praise their actions in the name of a national ideology of the "will" of the people. Neither has the ARF recognized that it has broken the law in more ways than one, because it believes all is done in the name of a higher vision, the creation of one nation and one homeland.

Whatever the deficiencies of the systems in Armenia and Karabagh, these two entities have at least definable political boundaries within which presidents and their administrations function effectively. They can speak on behalf of their constituencies, they can sign agreements and deliver what they promise, whether as policy or resource.

The Diaspora does not have a legal or otherwise agreed-on system to violate. The Diaspora does not have anyone who can speak for it. The legitimacy of power of those who claim to speak on its behalf is self-declaratory, but not self-evident. It is taken for granted, and it is not challenged in any forum. A state pro-

vides geographic and legal boundaries to contain disunited elements; regardless, "disunited" elements still remain citizens and
pay their taxes, and the president of Armenia or Karabagh can
still speak on their behalf and commit resources to achieve a
commonly agreed-on purpose. In a diaspora, challenges to political parties dissipate because the diaspora does not have such
boundaries. In diaspora communities the political space is occupied by ideals that are legitimized by tradition and self-preservation and are then used to equate all deviation with anti-national,
anti-unity sentiment.

However wide party memberships are spread across many
communities in the Diaspora, political parties do not reflect the
composition of this diverse Diaspora. Whatever the internal
mechanisms, leaders of political parties and major organizations
are assumed to have been selected by a process agreed on by the
members: Such leaders may, therefore, speak for their parties.
But the three traditional parties together represent an extremely
small fraction of the general Diasporan population. Diasporans
involved in organizations, not just political parties, number anywhere from zero to possibly as high as 40 percent, but is usually
not higher than 20 percent. That is still a minority. More important, much of the flaunted human and financial resources in the
Diaspora are not managed or directed by these organizations.

Furthermore, organizations with large memberships (churches,
the AGBU, and others) are nonpolitical and do not claim to speak
for the Armenian nation. It is not in their mandate to address
political agenda items and choices.

There are two ways to obtain legitimacy and to speak for the
nation in the Diaspora. One is the method of direct democracy:
elections for leadership of a community involving the highest
possible percentage of Armenians in that community.

Of the Diaspora communities, to my knowledge only those in
Hungary and Turkey have mechanisms to select a leader through
direct and general elections. Armenians in Hungary, by state law,
elect a leadership, the most recent exercise being in 1998. In
Turkey, the Patriarch of Istanbul is both the spiritual and civic

head of the community. By Turkish law, he is selected through a general election involving Turkish-Armenian citizens belonging to the Apostolic church, the absolute majority of Armenians in that country. In 1998, the most recent election for a Patriarch, Archbishop Mesrob Mutafian received over 90 percent of the vote in an election in which an unusual 50 percent or so of 35,000-plus eligible voters participated. Patriarch Mutafian can speak for the Armenian community of Turkey, even if by the same state law the leader of the community must be selected from among clergymen. With the possible exception of very small communities of a few families, nothing elsewhere comes close to this kind of legitimacy.

Even in Hungary and Turkey, however, where the mechanism exists for some kind of election, there is no election in any Diaspora community where candidates run for office on issues related to the present and future of Armenia or to the different ways to resolve the Karabagh problem or to indicate preferences for Armenia's social, political, or economic system. Elections of Armenians to designated seats in the Lebanese, Iranian, or Cypriot parliaments do not present the local Armenian with choices on such issues, even if votes may indicate a preference for one candidate or party over another.

The second method of achieving legitimacy is to create a forum of organizations and, on the basis of a formula that also allows the representation of the large number of individuals not associated with organizations, to approximate the will of the community. Diaspora communities have made no move in this direction. Individuals claiming to represent the "people" or "community" are not ready to test their claims through such a mechanism, to subordinate their institutional identities, traditions, individual positions, and organizational egos to a body that may be more inclusive; they are not willing to submit their programs to the scrutiny of the Diasporan in whose name and on whose behalf they pursue their policies.

Traditional political parties would also have to end their secretiveness, if they wish to become vehicles for the expression of any popular will. Demanding and zealous when it comes to democracy in Armenia, Armenian political parties in the Diaspora have maintained the nontransparency and secretiveness that characterized their activities in the Ottoman Empire. They provide no explanation for the adoption of policies or for changes in their policies or leaderships. This reflects a political culture based on entitlements, as if popular will is a loot to be shared, each share to be protected but not revealed. In this respect Diaspora political organizations have little to contribute to democracy and to political discourse in Armenia, however fragile, faulty, and imperfect Armenia's institutions may be.

Some organizations, even parties, may rethink these issues. But this would be a difficult proposition for those parties and organizations that base their legitimacy not on a democratic principal but on the claim that they "embody" the nation and the national will already.

Unity can serve a useful purpose if it begins with the recognition of and respect for differences: differences between Armenia and the Diaspora; differences in political environments, cultures, and subcultures; and differences in institutional and collective needs. Unity sought or achieved through the universalization of one's own worldview and its imposition on others are most impractical even dangerous bases by which to achieve national goals.

GENOCIDE AND THE POLITICS OF GENOCIDE RECOGNITION

The problem of the Armenian Genocide and the politics of its recognition need to be addressed in some detail. Having affected Diasporan thinking, the problem—in its Diasporan version—has now been introduced in Armenia.

I begin by enumerating what, for the purposes of this discussion, is *not* the problem in the Armenian Genocide and its recognition.

The problem is not the factuality of the Genocide. It did take place, whether anyone else recognizes it or not. The problem is not its calamitous consequences. The massacres and deportations between 1915 and 1917 were probably the most devastating event in the history of the Armenian people. They resulted in the deaths of probably more than a million Armenians and the deportation of at least that and many more and have impacted generations in ways known and unknown. The Genocide also resulted in the elimination of the Armenian indigenous people from a major part of its historic homeland.

The problem is not the exact figures, however important such numbers are for history. By any definition, it was genocide; the fact that some survived and others were not touched does not make it less of a genocide, less severe and traumatic, and less catastrophic. It is a wound that refuses to heal and that manifests itself in renewed ways.

The problem is not even the fact that, despite all the significance that the Diaspora and, beginning in 1965, Soviet Armenian authorities ascribed to that event, there has been no comprehensive and systematic effort commensurate with and worthy of the significance that of the event to properly document and explain it, valiant efforts by some individual scholars and groups notwithstanding.

The problem is not, furthermore, the motivation of those who wish to see the Genocide recognized. Obviously, there is a real need in the Armenian people to seek justice through the recognition by Turkey and the international community of the tragedy that befell them. I recognize the genuine interest of many non-Armenians—scholars, clergymen, and politicians—to see justice done. I also do not question the sincerity of political leaders who have labored and still do so on behalf of that cause just as I do not recognize anyone's right to question my motivations; I do not feel the need to establish my credentials in that painful arena.

The problem, moreover, is not the significance of this Genocide for Turkish history in particular and for history in general. Some Turkish scholars have begun to recognize the impact of the Armenian Genocide on Turkish politics, political thinking, and state-building. The Armenian Genocide is important for world history not because it is the first, as it is not, but because it is the model of a political genocide.

The problem is the place of the Genocide and of Genocide recognition in Armenian political thinking on three interrelated levels: in Armenian collective consciousness, in relation to other compelling issues within an Armenian political agenda, and in the international arena in which most problems of interest to Armenia and Armenians are being defined and contextualized.

Collective Consciousness

The memory of the Genocide is part of every Armenian's consciousness. Its nonrecognition constitutes a denial of a good part of Armenian identity, individual as well as collective. Armenians have difficulty understanding the world and accepting its laws and values as theirs, if the world cannot manage to recognize the obvious.

But the politicization of Genocide recognition and its centrality in Armenian political discourse with the rest of the world have had more of an impact on Armenians than on the world. Armenian history has been reduced to two periods: the pre-Genocide and the post-Genocide. Consequently, all that happened before 1915 must be interpreted as leading to 1915, and all that followed is the result of 1915. Thus, the long and complex history of the Diaspora has been simplified, and the Diaspora itself has been viewed as the consequence of the Genocide, making it difficult to fathom another politics, another future. It seems that Armenians no longer just live or understand, but they also glorify the psychology of the victim and cannot imagine alternatives.

The transformation has been intellectually paralyzing, politically debilitating, and psychologically humiliating.

That is not yet the case in Armenia, although a majority of Armenians there trace their origins to Western Armenia: to refugees from the Armenian provinces of the Ottoman Empire following the Russo-Turkish wars of 1827–1828 and 1877–1878, to survivors from the Genocide, and to repatriates from the Diaspora in 1946 and 1947, who were themselves survivors of the Genocide.

Just as it happened in the Diaspora, on the fiftieth anniversary of the Genocide in 1965, the new generation in Armenia could no longer contain the anger that the survivors themselves were too humiliated to feel. As an alternative to the official commemoration by the state and the Communist Party, students took to the streets of Yerevan. Crowds chanted "Our lands," referring to demands for territorial demands from Turkey. And the demonstrators were duly jailed. At exactly the same time, in the United States, the ARF expelled some student members of its youth organization who organized demonstrations against the Turkish mission at the United Nations.

In the wake of these events, a number of Soviet Armenian historians devoted their time to writing about the Genocide, although most their works were descriptive and repetitive. They were allowed to write, and the Soviet Armenian government was permitted to build a monument dedicated to the memory of the victims of the Genocide. The subject was no longer taboo as long as historians at the end of their journey through the sufferings of the victims would thank the Soviet Union, the Communists, and the Russian people for saving Eastern Armenians the fate of their brothers and sisters on the other side of the border. Articulation of anti-Turkish feelings was accepted as long as it did not lead to Armenians taking matters into their own hands.

For a decade or two the externalization of the anger as the purpose of politics and as national agenda worked itself out both in Armenia and in the Diaspora, peacefully as well as violently. A reassessment of the role of the Genocide and its recognition started eventually in Armenian political thinking. The process of reassessment and any new conclusions some reached were lost in the ever-widening concentric circles of the Diaspora discourse. Diasporas are, indeed, immune to revolutions, especially of the intellectual kind; they are intrinsically conservative and focused on preservation and are therefore attracted and beholden to the past.

Reassessment in Soviet Armenia took a different route. The students had many years to think about the future of Armenia. A number of groups evolved, with a variety of conclusions. Some decided that Genocide could not be the basis of political consciousness or foreign policy. Levon Ter-Petrossian, Vazgen

Manukian, and Babken Ararktsian, all of whom traced their roots to towns and villages in the Ottoman Empire, were at the forefront of these activities. Ter-Petrossian was briefly jailed in 1966 for his continuing activities.

To this day the people in Armenia remember their victims in a less political atmosphere than is the case in the Diaspora. Every April 24 they march silently to the Monument, pile their flowers around the eternal flame, and return to their homes. Silently, with no speeches. In the past three decades, no one has been allowed to personalize the pain and turn it into political capital. Now there are attempts to change that, too, in Armenia.

Making Genocide recognition the basis of all politics has led to an obsessive pattern of behavior. This behavior pattern has disabled the Armenian psyche and mind and, even worse, has made them hostage to the stimuli of others. Once more Armenian minds and thoughts have become hostage to Turkish policy, this time of denial, and to the vagaries of international recognition. Armenians are engaged in a protracted battle, the key to which is held by the "enemy." The state responsible for the Genocide and death still holds in its hands the health of the nation, this time its mental, psychic, and political health.

A Turkish Ambassador whom I met a few months ago in a third country insisted on engaging me in a discussion on what he termed the "so-called Genocide." My reflexive reaction was to oblige and argue the point. But I realized that yet again, I would have had to accept a discourse imposed by someone else; once more the Armenian had to prove something to the other person. I told him I did not wish to engage him on that subject; I did not think he was qualified to discuss that subject with me either as a scholar or a private citizen, that nonrecognition of the Genocide by Turkey said something about Turkey rather than about the Genocide. I refused him and the Turkish state the right to set my agenda once more, as they had that of my parents and grandparents. Nonrecognition was Turkey's problem, and I could not allow him or Turkish state policy to define my thinking, my agenda. I was a private citizen and could say what I wanted. I knew, of course, that Turkish state policy was only half the problem.

There must be another way of defining the issue and fighting the battle than giving Turkey the key to the Armenian agenda. Making denial the central and fundamental element in collective consciousness and political agenda is to allow, once more, a Turkish state policy to hold our people captive and to incapacitate them. Some leaders, including academics, seem to believe that the deeper one's feeling of being a victim, the better the argument for recognition; that the longer collective consciousness is guided by pain, the better the service to the cause.

Denial is clearly a matter of policy. It is policy for the U.S. government and for much of the media in the West. It was not always so; it became so. An analysis of the reasons that major Western newspapers, which routinely recognized the Genocide until 1975, changed their view since could be very enlightening. As much as Turkish attitudes too are to a large degree reflexive, denial is Turkish state policy. Reflexive actions that may make us feel good are not adequate responses.

Armenians have begged enough, have been humiliated enough, have been victims long enough. Genocide recognition by Turkey and the international community cannot be the only way Armenians can recover their identity and pride. At the end, the cure to the wound may be worse than the wound itself.

Documentation and research on the subject are essential, just as are understanding the event and placing it in the context of Armenian, Turkish, and world history. These activities deserve more support from the community than they have so far received. International recognition, including recognition by Turkey, must be part of the agenda. But the fragmented, impulsive, uncoordinated, and often thoughtless processes must be thought out, the current methods must be adjusted to the new realities in the Armenian world, and a more productive strategy must be considered.

Genocide Recognition on the Political Agenda

Could the Genocide continue to occupy the same place in Armenian political consciousness and could the battle for its recognition remain the same once Armenia became independent? Can the same role be assigned to them with the fate of Karabagh hanging in the air? Can "reflexive reaction" be the basis of foreign policy and the context within which the social and economic development of the people of Armenia and Karabagh will take place?

It would be interesting to explore the relationship between recognition of the Genocide by legislative bodies of various countries and other items on the agenda of Armenia and Armenians in the post-Soviet period. As soothing as such recognition is for every Armenian, the impact and significance of these acts remain to be understood and explored.

Conventional wisdom has a tendency to categorize countries that provide any recognition to the Genocide as "pro" Armenian. The classification of countries as "pro" or "anti" Armenian is a figment of Armenian imagination, which some politicians, within and outside the community, are happy to sustain. It becomes possible to sustain this jargon when Armenians position themselves as beggars who are happy with crumbs and when Armenians expect too much and, as beggars, are satisfied with very little— the choice of what to give belonging to the giver.

What happens to an Armenian issue when it enters the world arena, when it becomes part of the agenda of others? How much control do Armenians retain over their own agenda? What happens to an Armenian issue when it enters the arena of foreign policy and vital interests of major powers? The least one has to recognize is that, beyond the good will and humanitarian concerns of some political leaders and parties, countries and organizations assess the value of Genocide recognition in the context of their own relations with Turkey.

One is reminded of the pattern of relations between the Great Powers and the Ottoman Empire in late nineteenth and early twentieth centuries, at the height of Western imperialism: raise the issue of "the mistreatment of Armenians" sufficiently to obtain concessions for themselves and then leave Armenians hanging, figuratively and literally. Meanwhile, Armenians have raised their hopes, sometimes their guns, and Ottoman guns would be turned against the Armenians.

Equally important is the corollary to the logic described above: The premise in Armenian political thinking that what is bad for Turkey is good for Armenians. In the less-than-coherent and fluid world of international relations and in a region in which the two countries are and will remain neighbors, it is difficult to imagine that Armenia and Turkey do not or cannot have common interests.

Finally, what if having normal diplomatic and economic relations with Turkey is in the interest of Armenia as well as of Karabagh? Would not improved Armeno-Turkish relations weaken the Azerbaijani negotiating position, the rigidity of which is based on a policy of strangling the Armenian economy? Should the answer to these questions be positive, (and they might very well be when considered with some detachment, if merely considering the option is not labeled as treacherous), then the normalization of relations with Turkey would facilitate Armenia's role as a transit route of Caspian Sea hydrocarbon resources. Many "pro-Armenian" countries, which are encouraging Armenians to follow their anti-Turkish instincts, are competing to get the pipeline themselves. The problem for them is not to keep Azerbaijan from developing its resources and getting wealthy; rather, it is to share in that wealth. Problematic relations between Armenia and Turkey as well as between Armenia and Azerbaijan would make it difficult for Armenia to be part of the pipeline system and for the pipeline to go through the south Caucasus in general.

There have been two approaches to the issue of Genocide recognition. One approach expects recognition of a historical event as a form of moral obligation, as a matter of justice to history, as a necessity for healing. Another approach, usually offered by the political parties, views Genocide recognition as a first step toward reparations, including territorial reparations by Turkey. It should be obvious that if the consequence of recognition would be the loss of territory or even the raising of the issue of territorial reparations, Turkey has every reason to pursue the policy of denial and to do so vehemently, as it has done in the past. In this scenario, the second part of the program ensures that the first part will never be acceded to.

Moreover, the strategy of obtaining recognition has focused on convincing the international community—usually the legislatures of various countries, international and regional organizations, and non-governmental organizations. The logic is that once convinced, the international community would compel Turkey to recognize the Genocide. This logic has four problems. First, it is not the absence of knowledge of history that has delayed recognition. Second, the issue is not important enough for anyone in the international community to press Turkey, except in the manner indicated above. Third, the international community does not have adequate resources to compel Turkey on such matters. Fourth, Turkey has successfully resisted international pressure on much more immediate and critical issues. Its reaction to external pressure is, usually, a stiffer response.

For all its vehemence and devotion, the drive for Genocide recognition has had limited success internationally. As for Turkey, its policy of denial has become more official and more deeply rooted over the past decades.

If the purpose of obtaining recognition of the Genocide is to obtain recognition by Turkey as a matter of moral and historical justice, then the strategy may require rethinking. If the purpose of recognition by Turkey is anything beyond that, then the prospect of never obtaining it could be accepted as a minor failure, as long as some other purpose is achieved. What Armenians need to understand is that these "other" purposes, legitimate or not, eliminate or lessen the possibility of a reversal in Turkish policy of denial; they also diminish the credibility of the argument with the international community.

However novel or paradoxical this may sound, there was more progress on the issue of Genocide recognition during the last five years of the Ter-Petrossian administration, when a constructive dialogue had started with Turkey, than during the last three decades of anti-Turkish campaigns. Two public events stand out. The first is the participation in 1995 of a Turkish sociologist in the officially sponsored international conference on the eightieth anniversary of the Genocide in Yerevan, and that scholar's clear characterization of the events of 1915 as genocide. The second event was the visit of the Mayor of Esenyurt, a city near Istanbul, to Yerevan and to the Martyrs Monument. Only the naive and the guardians of orthodoxy could believe that such events happen without the acquiescence from the Turkish government.

Curiously, neither event was given much attention in the Armenian media or by people who claim to place Genocide recognition at the top of their agenda, political parties and scholars alike. The latter included some people who renewed their support of U.S. President Bill Clinton's candidacy to a second term in 1995, when he had reneged on his promise to recognize the Genocide during his first campaign in 1991. This was not the first time that Genocide recognition had been relativized by the guardians of the faith. Obviously, they permitted themselves to decide when and where to deviate from orthodoxy. The elected President of Armenia was denounced for doing less than that.

The recognition of the Genocide was one change that President Kocharian introduced in his agenda of discussions with Turkey. Two reasons might have been to make Armenia more sensitive to the needs of the Diaspora and to make the Diaspora more supportive of Armenia. Another motivation may have been to use the Genocide as a counter-weapon against Turkey, hoping the issue would temper Turkey's support for Azerbaijan in the Karabagh conflict. Still, the Kocharian administration did not make the recognition of the Genocide by Turkey a precondition for the normalization of relations with Turkey. Armenia still supports the policy of establishing diplomatic relations with Turkey without preconditions.

It is doubtful that the change of policy brought us closer to a Turkish recognition of the Genocide. Whether this change achieved any other purpose remains to be seen. Kocharian's priority remains clear: moving the economy of Armenia. The Diaspora is an important dimension of that goal; raising the issue of Genocide recognition is an important concession to the Diaspora. Opening the borders with Turkey is also essential for the same purpose; recognition by Turkey, therefore, was not made a precondition. Time will tell whether such eclecticism has produced or will produce any results.

5.

The Diaspora and Its Discontents

For friend and foe alike, when it comes to an inventory of political weapons, the Diaspora has been considered one asset that the Armenian side has and the Azerbaijani side does not. Along with unity, the Diaspora has a strategic value in the thinking of leaders in Karabagh and Armenia. It has assumed a significant role in the program of some political parties.

When Diasporan parties reinjected themselves into the politics of Armenia and Karabagh, wittingly or not they staked a claim on the role of ensurers of Diasporan support for Armenia and Karabagh. In some cases, they assumed political responsibilities vis-à-vis Armenian authorities, who count on them for economic and political support.

THE DIASPORA UNTIL 1988

The Armenian Diaspora is one of the most resilient and, according to some people, one of the best organized in the world. It has adjusted to different times and political and cultural spaces; it has refused to die, despite predictions; it has developed institutions and organizations to care for its needs.

Part of the explanation for its resilience lies in the fact that Armenians began leaving their homeland centuries ago and have continued doing so till our day, albeit at different paces and for different reasons. Above all, the term *Diaspora* is a negative definition. It refers to a group of people who are *not* where they once were and, in a manner of speaking, where they should have been, at least if the nation-state structure is accepted as the norm.

The other reason is that in the face of Genocide, Diaspora vigor has become a means to assert Armenians' rejection of their death sentence in 1915. It is the refusal to be sent to oblivion, a statement against forgetting.

Although it preceded the Genocide, the Armenian Diaspora recovered from the humiliation of deportations, which came to characterize the dispersed remnants of a people after 1915. Refugees arrived in countries whose languages they did not know, to whose cultures they were essentially alien, and whose indigenous people, while hospitable, also displayed the all-too-common prejudices toward newcomers. It was the "sal Arménien" (dirty Armenian) in France, the "starving Armenian" in the United States, the "Turko" (the Turk) in South America, the "sha'fet Arman" (a piece of an Armenian) in some Arab countries. Three generations of hard work, devotion by hundreds and thousands of individuals, economic integration, and the slow rebuilding of community were needed to overcome the psychological damage.

As strange as it may seem to outsiders, for the refugees sitting at interminable meetings of community organizations and endless discussions of the most trivial of issues was an act of self-assertion, of the creation of a sense of community, of being together and making decisions for one's group, even if these refugees had difficulty understanding the larger historical events that had affected them so profoundly. Listening to speeches made up of words they hardly understood and to sermons regarding a Christianity they could no longer comprehend, day by day, one by one, the survivors returned to life, adjusted to new environments, and co-opted the horrible memories of their dear dead. Most Armenians have now overcome much of that and have good reason to be proud of their rejuvenation.

But can we speak of one Diaspora, and can the Diaspora play the role it is assigned by some and claimed by others?

Differences That Matter

There are no accurate figures for the number of Armenians in the Diaspora. Four to five million is a fair estimate of the range, although some writers claim the figure to be as high as eight million.

Communities vary greatly in size and are dispersed over five continents, with main concentrations in Russia (close to one million), the United States (around one million), Georgia (around 450,000), France (around 350,000), the Near East (almost 400,000), and South America (more than 100,000), largely in Argentina.

Communities vary also in their origins and histories. Some communities, such as those in Northern Iran or in Anatolia, trace their origins to the formation of the Armenian nation. Most were settled before the Genocide, but replenished by it. Others still, such as Montreal, Sydney, and Melbourne, became communities only during the 1950s. They represent different stages of assimilation and acculturation. Consequently, communities have varying degrees and types of organized life.

Communities also differ in legal status within host countries. In Turkey and other Near Eastern countries that are inheritor states of the Ottoman Empire, the state provides a legal definition of the Armenian, and under the law communities have legal standing and some privileges, as well as some restrictions. In Western societies the relationship with the state is defined through the concept of the individual citizen.

Moreover, many Armenians who are technically Diasporans would not define themselves as such. Armenians in Moscow especially, but also those in some other parts of the former Soviet space, would have difficulty thinking of themselves as Diasporans. There was the USSR, a single homeland, of which Moscow was the capital and of which they were residents. How could they be Diasporans? Tbilisi and Istanbul gave birth to modern Armenian culture and many of its institutions. Armenians in Javakhk are too close to Armenia to feel like Diasporans. Most recent arrivals from Armenia and Azerbaijan also would have trouble identifying themselves as Diasporans. Though physically away, they have not yet really left Armenia or Azerbaijan. For those already assimilated with or even without vague memories of their ethnic origins, being a Diasporan lost its meaning long ago.

The Armenian Diaspora has been a constantly shifting phenomenon within itself. Having settled first in the Near East and Eastern Europe, many survivors of the Genocide or their offspring in the host country continued on to other countries, mainly to the United States, Canada, Australia, and Europe. Relations between different waves of settlers have not reflected a sense of oneness. Antagonisms, mutual distrust, dislike, and prejudice have been more characteristic of subgroup relations. Organizational structures often reflect these divisions.

The institutional structure of communities has successfully resisted change. Some organizations are on their way out, such as compatriotic unions that have preserved the memory of Western Armenian cities and villages. Very few new organizations have managed to attract and keep sufficient followers long enough for them to take root. The Armenian Secret Army for the Liberation of Armenia (ASALA), one of the few to have claimed a political agenda, managed to survive for a decade. Other than some professional societies, the Armenian Assembly of America (AAA) is the only one that overcame the obstacles to creating a new national organization in the Diaspora. Even the AAA was unable to expand into Canada and Europe.

Nonetheless, the history of the Diaspora has recorded a number of changes. Cities that constituted centers of Diasporan life have emerged and faded many times. Paris and Boston replaced Istanbul and Tbilisi after the Genocide, until the 1950s when Cairo, Aleppo, and then Beirut claimed primacy. Some writers suggest that by the 1990s, by its sheer numbers and intensity of community activities, Los Angeles should be considered the center of the Armenian Diaspora.

This change has not signaled a dominance of American Armenians. Most institutions, whether in North America or even in Europe, are still led by Armenians from Syria and Lebanon. This is quite important for understanding the content and form of the political and cultural program of the Diaspora. As the homeland has receded in memory, each generation has searched for what must be preserved from the past. And while no ideal or pure Armenian culture has ever existed or can exist, since the 1950s the Near Eastern, increasingly the Aleppo-Beirut model, has been promoted as the ideal, making people from that part of the world a natural elite for the leadership of communities worldwide. As a result, a hierarchy of communities has evolved. If the Syrian-Lebanese communities rest at the top, then the Turkish-Armenian and those from Armenia are at the bottom of the hierarchy.

In countries where communities are most threatened by assimilation, often defined as the loss of the use of the Armenian language, preservation has often been equated with conservative social values. As a result, liberal elements have often remained aloof from community institutions.

The result has been a kind of orthodoxy, at times intolerant and often exclusive; the tenets of this orthodoxy are known to the guardians of the faith. Communities have a centrifugal character: Members of the community who disagree with institutional policies and social values can leave and end their active participation. If this happens in an Armenian state, one still remains Armenian as well as a citizen of the country; in most Diaspora communities, such individuals disappear into the host citizenry, leaving Diaspora leaderships unchallenged. Some become active in less demanding community organizations. Few try to begin alternative organizations, and still fewer succeed.

The agenda of the Diaspora has changed, too. In the immediate post-Genocide and post-Sovietization atmosphere, the Diaspora was busy attending to its wounds. Most survivors made new homes; found a means of living; helped start schools, churches, and centers; and offered assistance to new refugees. They also had to answer questions such as how were Western Armenia and independence lost, who was responsible for these losses, and what to think of Soviet Armenia. All this was enough for anyone's plate; it consumed political debate in the first decades following the Genocide. Political debate degenerated into Cold War terminology in the 1950s. As if one's own wars were not enough, Armenian political parties made someone else's conflict as their own. During the brief 1958 civil war in Lebanon, Armenian political parties took sides, internalized the local conflict, which itself reflected Cold War positions, and killed each others' members.

Once it became clear that neither Western Armenia nor independence was coming back, the Diaspora was consumed by the danger of what was called the "white massacre," assimilation whose most telling evidence was the limited ability of the new generation in Western countries to use the Armenian language proficiently. Knowing Armenian and some rudimentary facts about Armenian history became the license to community leadership.

Equally important for understanding Diaspora-Armenia relations is the shifting meaning of the *homeland*. For many people and their offsping who survived the massacres and the Genocide in Western Armenia, homeland was Kharpert, Erzerum, or Van. Yerevan would not do. Most survivors of the Genocide from Cilicia could think only of their cities there—Adana, Marash, and so on—as their homeland. Few had much to do with the First Republic or imagined present-day Armenia—whose people spoke a different dialect and used a different orthography, not to speak of the mores—as their homeland.

This was particularly true in the American Armenian community, whose formation preceded the Genocide, with its thousands of workers from Western Armenia who hoped someday to go back. It was difficult to think of what had remained of Armenia as "homeland," particularly if one had ARF sympathies and when Yerevan was the capital of a Soviet state that replaced independent Armenia in 1920.

Acceptance of Soviet Armenia as "the homeland" was achieved with the help of two intermediate notions. First, Armenia was abstracted and idealized; it became an idea and a museum. Second, the 30,000 kilometer square space was only a temporary state: Someday, somehow, the other Armenia would be restored.

Then there is the economic dimension. Over time, Diasporans also improved their economic situation, although there are still pockets of poverty in various countries. By and large Diaspora Armenians do well economically. Moreover, Armenians give to their community institutions. There is wealth in the Armenian community. But it is important to distinguish between Armenian wealth and the wealth of Armenians. Armenians may be doing well, but very few Armenian institutions do well and few have endowments to keep them going.

This has been true historically. Wealthy Armenians usually give enough to organizations to sustain them, but few will endow organizations in a manner that will make these institutions independent. Maybe that is the way it should be. But people who do not understand this difference may see behind an organization's statements of support for Armenia dollars that are simply not that organization's to give.

Major Diasporan organizational budgets have increased from the thousands into the millions of dollars. Yet, except for the few that had endowments, ranging from a few million, such as the Armenian Relief Society (ARS) and the AAA to about a hundred million for the Armenian General Benevolent Union (AGBU), most income is collected annually; fund drives are usually successful when organized for specific projects, usually for buildings.

Foundations established by benefactors such as Calouste Gulbenkian in Lisbon, Alex Manougian in Detroit, and Kirk Kirkorian in California contribute substantially to Armenian life, but they are private and not community foundations; these foundations also help charities and culture in their adopted countries.

Overarching and Transstate Institutions

Against the deepening fragmentation of the Diaspora stood a number of organizations that transcended the boundaries of host states, when the latter increasingly defined the internal world and external environment of the refugee.

The most pervasive of those was the Apostolic Church, founded at a time when Armenians had kings. When the line of kings came to an end, the Church assumed more and more public and political institutional functions in Armenian life, possibly because the occupying powers assigned such functions to it.

In the Ottoman Empire, non-Muslims were made part of the state through the "millets," or religious communities. By state law and politics, the Church became the institution through which the state dealt with Armenians as Armenians. When recognized by law, the millet provided formal protection and set limits. The Church was the mediator between state and community, between conqueror and conquered. It had political responsibilities with extremely limited political rights. The cautious attempt by Patriarch Mkrtich Khrimian in the 1860s to increase those rights and turn the National Assembly representing the millet in Istanbul into a body representing the interests of the majority of Ottoman Armenians (the rural poor and downtrodden of the provinces rather than the relatively secure and well to do of the capital), was easily stopped by the Sultan and the privileged in Istanbul. The Church's failure was the main reason for the rise of the political, revolutionary parties.

On the Eastern side of the homeland, the Russians, then the Soviets, used the Church equally effectively as a more indirect means of control and containment. In both cases the Church—the oldest surviving institution in Armenian life—was transformed into a form of identification that by and large precluded its being used against the state.

Since the Genocide, the Church has continued to be a form of organization—intracommunity but suprastate—as well as a means of identification. It also took on the role of preserver of tradition and national identity, coming close to abandoning its original role as provider of spiritual and moral guidance. In the Diaspora, the Church was manipulated and controlled by antagonistic political parties, including those taking opposing sides during the Cold War.

Throughout history, the more the Church has assumed a "national" character and taken on nonspiritual and nonreligious functions, the more it has had to adjust to and accommodate political structures, Armenian or foreign.

The Armenian Catholic and Armenian Protestant churches have remained largely outside the internal battles, except in the mid-nineteenth century Ottoman Empire, when the Ottoman government decided to recognize them as separate millets. This institutional aloofness does not mean, however, that their leaders and members have not had sympathies, that they have not shared the fate of the rest of the nation, or that they have not brought their contribution to cultural and educational life.

Organizations such as the AGBU and the ARS have been instrumental in adding important dimensions to the transstate

sense of common bonds in the Diaspora. While themselves associated with political parties, these organizations have provided
excellent opportunities for members of the nation to come
together and, at the same time, help the less fortunate.

Some organizations, such as the Tekeyan Cultural Association
and the Hamazkaine Cultural Association, that were founded in
the Middle East as the cultural wings of political parties and
served a very useful purpose there, have failed to be as effective
in the United States, France, and Canada. In the Middle East,
these associations were vehicles of Armenian cultural transmis-
sion and encouragement of the arts and education; they also were
windows to the cultures of their countries and the world.

Political Parties in a Diasporan Setting

One odd phenomenon of the Armenian predicament is that
organizations calling themselves "political parties" function in
the Diaspora. This is not usually the case with other diasporas.

The three parties, the Armenian Revolutionary Federation
(ARF), the Armenian Democratic Liberal party (ADL), and the
Social Democratic Hunchakian Party (SDHP), were founded to
defend the cause of or to represent Armenians in the Ottoman
Empire. The Genocide had put an end to their activities in
Turkey; the Sovietization of the First Republic closed Armenia.
After 1921, they became Diaspora parties. These parties became
primarily organizations that helped build community institutions
and control them. They also shared, along with the Church, in the
task of representing the community at the level of the authorities
of the adopted country, in some cases within the set legal structures of that state, in others informally. The diasporization of
political parties occurred when these two functions filled most of
the time of the members of the organizations.

Then there was the third level of activity, what has been
loosely called *Hay Tahd*, Armenian Cause. The term *Armenian
Cause* evoked anything and everything that touched Armenians,
from identity crises to unity within the community, from the lack
of mechanisms to avoid mixed marriages to legitimizing Armenian history in universities, from the problem of generational con-

flicts to the Turkish denial of the Genocide and the battles for the international recognition of that Genocide.

Buried in the evolving definition of the Armenian Cause was the strictly political goal of creating the ideal homeland. Almost transcendental in its definition, the Armenian Cause was transformed gradually into a mythical battle with mystical strategies in a world of international affairs that few were privileged to know and still fewer still were expected to understand.

By the 1970s, the recognition of the Genocide became the key to understanding the Armenian Cause. Political parties linked the recognition of the Genocide and the dream of a greater Armenia. Turkey's recognition of the Genocide would constitute the legal basis for Armenian claims on Western Armenia, its eastern provinces. The political support would come from countries that also would have recognized the Genocide; practical support would come from the traditional enemy of Turkey, the Russians, and the USSR, which would accept a united Armenia but would be opposed to a free and independent one.

There was a time when the ARF wanted it all: a free, independent, and united Armenia, free and independent coming first until the 1960s. A free and independent Armenia was not just a fantasy, the ARF party argued; it was a distinct probability. The USSR would collapse soon of its own weight and anomalies. The anti-ARF camp wanted no part of that scenario, for fear of upsetting the USSR, to which Armenia was entrusted. When the ARF shifted its strategy (the "united" now having priority) and the anti-ARF parties thought it was possible to actively promote the idea of a united Armenia, a consensus was reached and the contemporary definition of the Armenian Cause was born and shared by the three traditional parties. The ideological and programmatic conflict between the ARF and the anti-ARF (ADL and SDHP) camps gradually disappeared, although the traditional antagonism survived. Meanwhile, the third level of activity, now too distant for a settled Diaspora, had been reduced to the problem of the recognition of the Genocide, a matter so sacrosanct that no Armenian could question without ensuring himself or herself a place in hell.

Yet there was not much discussion on any of the assumptions underlying the argument: that Turkey would recognize the Genocide knowing that it would be followed by demands of territorial reparations; that Western countries and NATO would accept or support the dismemberment of one of their members to the benefit of the rival against which NATO is directed; that the USSR would risk its position in the world security system and the multilayered relations it was developing with the West for the Armenians.

There had also been no evidence that the USSR wanted to endanger its relations with Turkey. For decades since the Bolshevik and Kemalist revolutions, the two nations had not engaged in war; they had avoided confrontation at all cost. Wisely, Turkey did not enter World War II. The only incident that might have led some people to think otherwise happened when toward the end of World War II the USSR raised the issue of Kars and Artahan, two districts in Turkey that were part of historic Armenia but, more important, part of the First Republic, 1918–1920. But the purpose of that maneuver was to give Turkey a scare and nudge it toward entering the war on the side of the allies. Besides, Georgians thought the issue was raised on their behalf, and the USSR never presented a formal demand for these territories to the Turkish government.

But these questions would only encumber the picture and could demystify the strategic game. The fact is that the highest ideal too was diasporized; it was understood in a manner that did not require answers and was nurtured through a process that was not expected to produce results. One party leader argued in 1987 that the value of the slogan of an independent Armenia was in its ability to motivate and inspire the youth. The longing for an independent homeland as an ideal was a statement about one's nobility of thought and spirit; it was not a program that required a credible strategy and results—in one word, accountability for actions, promises, and performance.

It is not surprising that Diasporan political discourse had expropriated the terminology of the Church: *hope, faith, sacrifice,* and *will* were the most common words in speeches and editorials. The international community was "immoral" and treacherous.

The Armenian Cause had become a form of religion, with its own hierarchy of sins and saints, party leaders having assumed the role of the intermediaries, the interpreters.

The ADL and SDHP had surrendered to history; their ideological structures need not have been so elaborate, the theology so refined. It was the ARF that had aimed the highest and had the most to prove. Had there been a procedure for accountability, the ARF would have had to explain its failure on the third level and, toward the end of the seven decades when it too accepted a non-free and nonindependent Soviet Armenia, its strategy to liberate the other parts of the homeland. But insulated from the day-to-day vagaries of political life, the ARF shrouded its actions and policies in mystical clouds, in concentric circles. Only the highest echelon members were privy to the intricacies of its belief system.

The heroes and martyrs whom the ARF had produced and would still produce entitled it to that presumption. From the first fedayees who sought death fighting Ottoman soldiers, to Soghomon Tehlirian and his friends who assassinated the authors of the Genocide, to the last of the "martyrs" in the Turkish Embassy in Lisbon in 1983, the ARF provided, as any religion should, the models of personal salvation.

The mysticism engulfed every member. Members of the ARF, and to a lesser extent members of other parties, felt a kind of bond that was difficult for nonmembers to comprehend. Members felt empowered; they were part of this tight and select brotherhood that had once defied the Ottoman and Russian empires, that had produced heroes and martyrs, created a republic, formulated the highest ideals of the nation, and preserved them in communities it governed on all continents. Armenians in places where it could not do so, such as in the USSR and Turkey, were not considered essential in the larger picture or for the strategy of the Armenian Cause. The USSR as a state, however, was reinvented as a partner in that strategy, one with whom one negotiated as an equal, while Turkey was recast in the role of the villain. Members wanted to believe that their parties influenced the behavior of many governments and aimed at creating and administering the best Armenia yet, an Armenia that would embody the best of a

3,000-year-old experiment, a sense of brotherhood that defied history and transcended the boundaries that mortals had created.

Parties offered a whole worldview that encompassed everything from the education of children to culture and sports and religion; from relations with host countries to international relations; from the definition of treachery to death by martyrdom, and to the promised afterlife. For ARF members especially, their party was the answer to all Armenian ills that came from history, to all problems facing Armenians now—wherever they may be and whatever the problems.

Could one ideology, one program, one organization be so many things, for so long, to so many people, in so many countries, and still be effective? Part of the answer is suggested by the question. When one has assumed so much responsibility, one expects the everyone else to understand and support but not criticize. In other words, this is the wrong question to ask, when one is dealing with identity, hope, and belief.

The other part of the answer is that in the deep, deep bowels of the party psychology what matters is that instinctive need for the Diasporan to be organized, the need that began with the failure of the Church in the Ottoman Empire to articulate the problems of the nation. The SDHP but especially the ARF had rejected the "religious minority" status and had been able to change the psychology of the Armenian from a servile third-rate citizen to one who considered his life, his cause, and his people important enough to give that life away, to become a fedayee, to become a martyr.

The survivor and the refugee also needed to prove he was still alive, alive as an Armenian and still able to act, however much history had come close to reducing him to nothingness.

Deep, deep down, more than an ideology, a political party, a program, or a strategy, the ARF is an organization. The highest principle for the ARF is the principle of its organization. It is difficult to find in history, with a few possible and interesting exceptions, a party that has spent and continues to spend so much time and energy on organizational rules. A combat-ready and well-honed organization can serve whatever the need, on whatever level, wherever. Programs may change, ideologies come and go, events pass by, history may deal a heavy blow, even a mortal one, Armenians may be facing the world and its major powers. But all is fine if the organization is there. Then a few people can build a church, open a school, plan a revolution, defend the community against physical attacks, make deals and compromises, and still dream of the ideal Armenia. Through organization, one person makes a difference. The organization is the repository of the strength of the nation, the masculinity of the nation, as one ARF historian characterized it.

To be able to make these shifts and changes, sometimes in basic principles, and still to be effective and survive, the organization needs discipline. Most intraparty issues or "inquisitions" of members within the ARF have dealt with violations of organizational rules; and ideological, programmatic, and policy battles, which flare up on a regular basis, are resolved through these rules.

In return for submission to organizational rules and discipline, the ARF empowered each of its members. The lowliest member was presumed, by the grace of membership, to represent the pure Armenian as well as the wisdom of the past. The one hundred years of experience was transmitted, it is believed, to each member, who was, by definition, better qualified to run a school, a church, a newspaper, a country because he represented collective and historic wisdom and will.

The ARF, with its devoted and believing members, has been one of the most important assets for a nation divided, dispersed, and threatened as a nonstate people. The party has been able to capture and articulate the anger, frustration, and dreams of a people that has received the deceptive sympathy of other nation but not much more.

The ARF has often been valiant and courageous. It was the arm of the nation that struck down those who organized the Genocide, when the world wanted to forget it. No Talaat Pasha should have gone unpunished. And when Soghomon Tehlirian struck Talaat down in Berlin, he did so in the names of not only those who had perished but also of those who survived and the descendants of those who survived, even if the world will not claim such an act as justice for all men. History sometimes does cross paths with justice. Sometimes history appears in the form of individuals. And when it does, the game is usually over; the deed is done.

But in the process, over the past seventy years, the ARF also evolved and became a state within the nation and within the community, at the same time as it has claimed the status of a trans-state national organization. That would, indeed, make it very difficult for the ARF to accept or be part of a more modest, a "normal" state, a "normal" Armenia. Unless, of course, the ARF was that state.

In the presence of such a formidable organization with such credentials and claims, the ADL and the SDHP assumed the role of the challengers. They, too, after all, were Armenian; they also had done great deeds; they had a following. The two parties tried to act as the antidote to ARF claims of hegemony.

In a 1982 lecture in Los Angeles, I argued that the "Armenian Cause" has two problems. The first was ARF members, who believed that being a member of the ARF was a condition necessary and sufficient to solve the Armenian Cause. The second were people who believed that being anti-ARF was the condition necessary and sufficient to achieve the same goal.

In one sense, the antagonism between the parties spurred competition for more and better institutions in the community. Yet the overpoliticization of the community may not have been a positive development. The community focused energies on petty power politics; it turned nasty and alienated a good portion of the new generations; it took quality away more often than not; it decreased the credibility of community leaders in the eyes of the majority of the noncommitted members who still have an impact; and it made the parties vulnerable to manipulation from host countries and other international forces.

At the end, momentous decisions were made, and cultural, political, and intellectual patterns were developed essentially by three organizations, whose combined world membership in 1988 numbered around 12,000; ARF represented nearly three-fourths of that number.

It is these "parties" that have injected themselves into the politics of Armenia and Karabagh on the ground, not just from afar as support mechanisms.

Achieving a Modus Vivendi

The recriminations and convulsions finally died down in the Diasporan world in the 1980s. The Cold War, adopted by the political parties and injected into community and Church affairs, had ended. The battles had been fought; Armenians had killed each other for the Cold War, the ultimate form of taking part in world affairs.

The last violent battle was fought between the ARF and the Armenian Secret Army for the Liberation of Armenia (ASALA), but that battle was over an issue on which everyone came to agree—the Genocide: Who was better equipped to pursue that agenda? Another, this time nonviolent, battle was fought between the political parties, mainly between the ARF and the Armenian Assembly of America (AAA). That too was settled.

The Diaspora was at peace, even content, with itself. Some intellectuals even started talking of a Diaspora as a "value" in itself, independent of a homeland, as a kind of permanent though "spiritual" home and not just a subject of analysis. This attitude was a form of resignation to the predicament as well as liberation. Now it was time, some people argued, to explore the existential meaning of being a Diaspora freed of the constraints that the "homeland" connection placed on it.

But at what cost was this modus vivendi achieved? A Diaspora at peace provided an opportunity for many organizations to focus on building institutions, on increasing the community's ability to impact their governments where this was permitted, and on providing some support to culture, arts, education, as well as on Genocide recognition efforts.

The battle for community control had been resolved, however, in one of two ways: by the control by one party at the exclusion of others or by dividing up the community into "spheres of influence" where each party was unchallenged. The question of

Church unity was resolved by each side making sure it kept control over its "Church," which meant ensuring a divided Church. Parties cooperated where they had to, but otherwise each left the other alone. Party organs stopped critiquing other parties; no real issues and controversies would see the light of day. Few questions were raised about the quality and content of schools and textbooks, quality and style of leadership, intracommunity tensions, strategies of pursuing the recognition of the Genocide, accountability of party and institutional performance, and other such matters. Parties and organizations were content to retain control over their spheres and to preserve the basis of financial and other support for their activities. Historians were proving, time and again, that the Genocide had occurred, and parties were pursuing the recognition of Genocide. There was not much left to think about.

The Diaspora also suffered from a sense of inertia and boredom. Its institutions had found a sense of balance, had defined the world in which they could function. The past was being accounted for and defended, the present was sailing along fine, and the future was quietly identified with the future of the countries where Armenians were living. But Soviet Armenia and Soviet Armenians were not part of all this.

For some organizations, Armenia merely existed—Soviet and imperfect and worth loving, even worth assisting in small ways, from afar. For others, the "homeland" was an idealized Armenia, an Armenia that did not exist and would probably never exist. But the investment was in the longing rather than in obtaining. For most, however, Soviet Armenia remained far, dotted by medieval monasteries and a Hellenistic temple, represented by pictures of grapevines and museums; Armenia was a museum—open air, but a museum nonetheless.

The Diaspora entered the fateful decade beginning in 1988 largely at peace, having avoided internal bloodshed during the Civil War that started in 1975 in Lebanon. It was fragmented but active, steeped in community politics, and self-contented.

THE DIASPORA FACES CHANGES ON THE "HOMELAND" FRONT

The mass demonstrations in Yerevan that erupted in February 1988 in support of Karabagh's demand for unification with Armenia shook the Diaspora. The demonstrations in Stepanakert were followed by the pogroms of the Azerbaijani city of Sumgait against the city's Armenian population and by the emergence of the Karabagh Committee. Then came the earthquake of December 1988 that shook much more than the earth.

In the summer of 1990 the ANM assumed power through elections, and in 1991 Armenia declared independence and created an executive presidency. From 1991 to 1994 the Karabagh political conflict became the Karabagh war, which was won by the Armenian side. Within a short period of time Armenia and the world had changed. How did the Diaspora react? How did it adjust to these changes, or did it?

The mass movement was, first and foremost, a surprise to the Diaspora. While very few held the Soviet system dear, it was unimaginable to challenge the government in the streets; and while not really understanding the scope and direction of the movement, Diasporans were in search of a "real" explanation and were at a loss when they thought of the consequences.

Some people, usually historians and those affiliated with the parties, knew where Karabagh was and what its problem entailed. Most did not. Yet, for the first time in decades, the world media, almost in awe, had an Armenian issue on the front pages and as their lead stories. The last time Armenians made news was during the 1973 to 1983 decade, when Turkish diplomats were assassinated by Armenian groups, and most Armenians were not sure they liked the image of the Armenian that was being projected. Now the international press was explaining where Armenia and Karabagh were.

For Diasporans in search of the acceptance of their identity, tired of explaining "what an Armenian was" to their neighbors, friends, and co-workers, thus attention was nothing short of a miracle.

They may not have been sure, however, that they welcomed this unannounced miracle. In one week, the people of Armenia, who had been counted out of history, had done what the political parties, lobbies, and cultural and academic organizations had not been able to do for decades.

The word *people* suddenly acquired a new, almost disturbing, meaning.

The pogroms in Sumgait, however, were more familiar events. One knew how to react. They evoked history and anger, the feeling of being once more a nation of victims. The pogroms reminded Armenians of some of the less friendly dimensions of the Soviet regime; they also reinforced the image of the "Turk" as the eternal enemy, the everpresent threat. But the movement continued. Yerevan and the Karabagh Committee had taken the leadership.

Diasporan political parties were in a difficult situation: They were scrambling to find explanations to offer to the public on momentous events that had received the world's attention but in which they had no role, and next to which all else was eclipsed. The parties were measuring events in terms of what Moscow would think and do, not really trusting that Armenia could produce a sustained political movement in pursuit of national goals of which they had been the guardians. For Diasporan Armenian political parties, the modus vivendi was not only within the Diaspora, but also between the Diaspora and the Soviet Union and, by extension, Soviet Armenian authorities: The Communist Party of the USSR ruled over Armenians in the USSR, and the Diasporan political parties governed the Diaspora.

On 1 October 1988, in a rare instance when they agreed on anything in writing, the ARF, the ADL, and the SDHP released a "Joint Statement." This statement constitutes one of the most important documents in the history of the last decade. Its last three paragraphs are worth quoting here:

We demand that the republican leadership in Soviet Armenia, placing an added resolve in becoming the legitimate interpreter of the rightful claims of the Armenian masses, adopt the Karabagh issue as their priority agendum striving to bring it to just and comprehensive solution, at the same time deeming unacceptable and incongruous with the claims of the people of Armenia all those initiatives brought to bear up to this point.

We also call upon our valiant brethren in Armenia and Karabagh to forgo such extreme acts as work stoppages, student strikes, and some radical calls and expressions which unsettle the law and order of the public life in the homeland and subject to heavy losses the economic, productive, educational and cultural life as well as the good standing of our nation in its relations with the higher Soviet bodies and also with the other Soviet republics. These zealous attitudes also provide the fodder for the ulterior motives of the enemies of our people.

Above all, we should safeguard the unity of our people, wherein lies our strength, and we should pursue our ultimate interests with farsightedness and determination.

The text requires no comments, though it does deserve close reading, in view of subsequent developments and the politics of the three parties. It is also worth noting that the Armenian text was released immediately, causing consternation in Armenia and Karabagh and in some circles of the Diaspora, including some members of the ARF. The ARF published the English translation, from which the above quotation is made, in the English insert of the ARF Buro's official organ in May 1989, while the imprisoned members of the Karabagh Committee were still awaiting trial in Moscow.

Then came the earthquake, which invited worldwide sympathy and compelled Mikhael Gorbachev to cut short his visit to the UN and fly to the scene. Gorbachev's visit to Armenia had more than a symbolic meaning.

First, Gorbachev promised to rebuild the ravaged area in two years and placed the cost at more than 14 billion U.S. dollars. The figure did not correspond to the evident abilities of Diasporan organizations, which, nonetheless, started providing assistance.

However important and well-advertised these contributions were, they could not finance the project of rebuilding, although a united effort could have eliminated much duplication and could have been more effective for Diaspora organizations that had no experience in disaster relief.

There were serious efforts to bring resources together. The SOS-Arménie and Charles Aznavour in France brought invaluable assistance, even if the result was not a fully integrated effort from within France. Pooling of resources occurred in the United States as well at the insistence of Kirk Kirkorian, who established the United Armenian Fund, which he funded generously hoping that it would bring about a commitment by major organizations to work together. The United Armenian Fund continues to work well and has been a major service in ensuring the transportation of donations, even though the initial aim of unity did not materialize, as participating organizations preferred to develop projects on their own and to make sure that their organizations received due credit and influence.

Second, Gorbachev told Armenians to forget politics and Karabagh and to think about rebuilding. Most Diasporans thought it was wise advice, only to be shocked when a survivor of the earthquake took Gorbachev to task in Leninakan, now Gumri, by asking him why he was not doing the right thing and allowing Karabagh to be united with Armenia.

Third, Gorbachev used the earthquake to send the members of the Karabagh Committee to a Moscow prison. Few in the Diaspora protested.

The earthquake produced less noticed consequences, too. Until the earthquake, to be useful to the community and, by extension, to the "nation" and "Armenia," one had to be an editor, a writer, a teacher, a clergyman or, a leader of any of the organizations, regardless of one's profession, with the possible exception of the historian. The only exceptions were benefactors, some lawyers who worked on cases of national significance, and historians, who became prominent and necessary as the defenders of the historical truth on the Genocide.

But earthquake relief needed doctors, pharmacists, and other medical workers, as well as engineers. The number of individuals in these professions who, in most cases individually or in small groups, provided immediate and long-term relief, is large. In France an existing organization of Armenian doctors assumed an important role. Similar groups were formed in North America and elsewhere. In addition to those already mentioned, a select group of individuals—Louise Simone Manougian and Hrair Hovnanian of the United States and Vache Manougian of the United Kingdom as well as others—brought invaluable assistance, personally and through organizations, and made a difference in the building of new Armenia in more ways than one.

With the advent of independence, this transformation continued and expanded to other professions as well; most of these individuals were unaffiliated with national organizations. The earthquake provided an opportunity to these organizations to co-opt the tremendous assistance Diasporan professionals could have provided, were ready to provide, and for the most part did provide during and long after the earthquake. Most of these professinals were looking for leadership within the organized community. But, generally speaking, most organizations were reluctant to adjust their operations, lest they lose control of operations, if not of the organization itself. Leaders of organizations insisted on making disaster-relief decisions on their own.

Finally, it was evident that the priorities of Diaspora Armenians in directing their financial contributions and human resources had also changed. Armenia now became the focus for many.

Then came independence. The ADL and SDHP accepted it immediately, as did the absolute majority of the Diasporans and Diaspora organizations.

The lone hold out was the ARF and its camp. The party that had kept the faith of an independent Armenia could not find it in its heart to accept independence. ARF members, the most ardent, if not overzealous, believers in that dream, were not permitted by the party to rejoice at the birth of an independent Armenia. Independence was not timely, the party argued; it was not a prudent move, it was "thrown" at Armenia, and not won. Independent Armenia was being managed by "a bunch of young, inexperienced leaders."

The dismal showing of the ARF candidate in the 1991 presidential elections shattered the illusion—pervasive among party members and sympathizers—that all that the people of Armenia needed was the choice of an ARF candidate to return the party to the leadership of the homeland. A number of prominent party members doubted the wisdom; of fielding a candidate so early; some were promised portfolios in the cabinet of the future ARF president.

After 1991 the ARF went to work within the community and with the host governments. The anti-Ter-Petrossian, anti-ANM, anti-government campaign, bordering on the anti-Armenia, did not bring down the government, but it justified subsequent illegal activities in Armenia. It poisoned the atmosphere in the Diaspora and confused many.

Thus, ideology became faith, and a blind faith needs hatred to sustain itself, to overcome any doubts that facts may inconveniently raise. And hatred is best served when personalized. Nothing Ter-Petrossian did could be right or could have a trace of wisdom, and every step he undertook pursued an evil purpose. In an article reproduced in many party organs, an ARF leader charged Ter-Petrossian of "stealing" the tricolor and the national anthem from the ARF and making them the flag and anthem of the new republic; he had already stolen the idea of independence and the country. What else would he steal if left unchecked?

ARF propaganda marked a new low in the politics of hatred. It involved a systematic, sustained vilification of the person who had been elected by the people of Armenia with 83 percent of the vote. In ARF newspapers, the first-ever elected president of the newly independent homeland was called names that others, from Bolsheviks to Young Turks, had been spared.

But it is difficult to determine what was worse: the organized and sustained ARF campaign to denigrate, almost dehumanize a President or the fact that no Diasporan leader or organization condemned such behavior publicly. Church leaders as moral authorities failed to do so; academics as guardians of the nation's history and intellectual leaders failed to do so; other parties, participants in the political discourse, failed to do so in the Diaspora. Many people were enraged. Yet, except for two, possibly three, lesser-known honorable columnists, such behavior went unchallenged. Regardless of the reasons, the phenomenon and the absence of a reaction say something about Diaspora politics and discourse. In some ways they reflect the disdain that exists among some Diasporans toward the people of Armenia. Let us imagine anyone using such words—say, a non-Armenian columnist writing in any newspaper—toward any second-echelon ARF leader. What would have been the reaction of the ARF, of other parties, of the community and its organizations, including those traditionally opposed to that party?

In some respects, that hatred was directed at an Armenia and, by extension, at its people who had dared change the course of history on their own, without asking the Diaspora. This was the dilemma of many Diasporans, of devoted members of organizations, despite the inner voice that sought the homeland, sought ways to express themselves and to act in support of the homeland.

But it is not easy to battle the realities around that dilemma. How could the safety found in the Diaspora, the political certainty of an ideology, the emotional security of a blind faith, and the un-challenging simplicity of an idealized homeland be supplanted by a real country whose people are poor and whose institutions are still being formed and tested by forces within and outside its control; whose men have fought battles and whose families have buried their men; whose women are battered by war, economy, and male chauvinism; whose artists, writers, and intellectuals now must struggle to make a living? How can reality fight fantasy, when fantasy is so removed and safe?

Insecurity and uncertainty cannot prevail as modes of life when an imagined history never provided such grim details, when history never talked of poor peasants, beggars and prostitutes, not only living, but also being part of the "homeland," of that magic word *Armenia*? And a "higher morality," nurtured by the psychology of the victim, cannot accept a strategy that is based on transcending that moralization and victimization. The intolerance of the blindly faithful and the faithfully blind cannot accept hard reality.

Then came the war that was started by a combination of USSR and Azerbaijani military units in 1991 and was very quickly transformed into an Azerbaijani-Armenian war. When the most recent and enduring cease-fire came in 1994, it was won by the Armenian side. Armenian forces had kept control not only of Nagorno Karabagh, but also of seven non-Armenian populated regions of Azerbaijan, including the strategic Lachin region. There were refugees on both sides, but mostly Azerbaijanis dislodged from these districts. The success of the war was assured by the people of Karabagh and Armenia. They tightened their belts, suffered the consequences of continuing blockades along with other deprivations, and sacrificed their sons and husbands. And they kept a country going and Karabagh safe for all to admire and be proud of. These are the same people, the same mothers and sisters, the same officials and civil servants whose morals, integrity, and dedication are often scorned publicly and unashamedly in some Diasporan newspapers by self-designated purist preachers.

The Diaspora could have helped financially, and it did. Many people gave more and in more ways than one, and remain unheralded.

As for the much publicized participation of Diasporans, suffice it to state that the number of Diasporans who left the Diaspora to fight in the war was 14: Ten were former members of the ASALA, two were ARF-ers, and two were independents. The rest of the fighters were the sons and daughters of Karabagh and Armenia Armenians. For the few among the latter who had political affiliations with Diasporan parties, fighting for Karabagh preceded their membership in parties, just as for many involved in the struggle against the Ottoman Empire before World War I, being a fedayee preceded and superseded their affiliation with organized revolutionary parties.

The outcome of the war gave the Diaspora a sense of pride and contentment. It had been a long time since Armenians had marked a victory on the battlefield. The close identification of

Azerbaijan with Turkey made Azerbaijan an extension of Turkey in the minds of the Diaspora Armenians. Some even felt good that they were seen by foreigners as the victimizer—a sense that competed for a moment, though not successfully in the long run, with the self-image of the victim. The occupation of Azerbaijani territories was also perceived by many Diasporans as the rightful revenge of the past. There are those who believe that the return of these territories would constitute treason.

Armenia, Karabagh, and the Diaspora or the many Diasporas have had ample opportunity to deal with each other, on a governmental level, institutionally, and individually. A decade of intense relations has provided time to all to disabuse themselves of idealized images of the other, of most of the unrealistic expectations.

Business people, who have much to contribute to Armenia's economy, have learned that one does not leave the kind of judgment and business acumen that made a successful capitalist at the border and make decisions on partners and investments while raising toasts to Ararat and Karabagh.

Diaspora Armenians have learned that Armenia is a real place, with real people, with real problems. It is not history; it is not a museum. It is not a place where romantic views and false assumptions survive; it is not the stuff of which dreams are inspired. It is as brutal as reality gets.

Many Diasporans did not like what they saw; they have not adjusted fully to Armenia's realities. What they did not like in Armenia they still seek to find in Karabagh: the pure, the traditional, the heroic, the comforting. Questions asked of Armenia and Armenian politics are rarely asked of Karabagh. The patriotism of Karabagh leaders is never questioned; those in Armenia remain guilty until proven to be only suspects.

Well organized or not, up to its potential or not, the Diaspora as a whole, through organizations and individuals, has contributed tremendously to Armenia and Karabagh. Some organizations, such as the AGBU and the Armenian Assembly of America (AAA), many Church organizations, including the Catholic and Protestant Armenian churches, a number of professional groups, and a huge number of individuals, using their positions in non-

Armenian institutions and organizations, brought that help. For many of these people that help was the first act of real involvement in the "Armenian" world, an involvement for which they had no motivation or forum before.

Some organizations engaged in rethinking their budget allocations, redistributing their efforts, and defining a realistic role for their organizations in Armenia. Those that did so early on, such as the AGBU, the AAA, and the Catholic and Protestant churches, escaped wrenching divisions and internal battles. Political parties and other organizations that did not do so consciously and realistically ended up with divisions, splits, and nagging internal struggles that only accentuated their problems and exacerbated relations with Armenia and Karabagh. All three political parties have suffered such consequences.

Regardless of the formal policy or behavior of organizations, for most Diasporans the differences between parties in the Diaspora and their battles, legitimate or contrived, have become almost absurd and irrelevant, the absence of unity in the Church even more so.

While political parties wondered how an independent Armenia plays within their claim to representation of the community and lobbying efforts in the host countries, what most Diasporan Armenians felt instinctively was the joy of having a country they could call Armenia, whose "flag flew at the UN." To be able to utter, and to hear from non-Armenian sources, expressions such as "The President of Armenia," the "Ambassador of Armenia," or "the Commander of the Armenian Army" became a source of deep pride, real satisfaction, and rejuvenation.

Armenians sensed that since the movement and independence, their children no longer ask, "What is Armenia?" or "What is an Armenian?" The battle for identity had been won, at least partly: The movement, independence, and the war had given Diaspora children something that money could not and, in fact, did not buy for decades.

Serious academics, intellectuals, and community leaders have realized that Armenia and Karabagh are not there to cause pride or embarrassment to the Diaspora, that the Diaspora should not project its agendas into these events, that this is not a game. They have come to understand that to the extent that there is a game, it is being played by major powers, who know the difference between national interest and ideology; between strategy and propaganda, between what is good and what feels good; that words uttered by an official of the government of Armenia make a difference for that country's relations with other countries and can have consequences, unlike the statements of Diasporan parties, which at best will enervate a country or two or will be manipulated by others.

Many Diasporans realized that letting Armenia decide its own fate is the wiser course: A course that was and is important for the Diaspora, but that had no real consequences on the lives of Diasporans, may have a different impact on the people of Armenia and Karabagh, and people directly affected should make those choices; that imposing the Diasporan agenda on Armenia is a mistake, unless the Diaspora is able to care for all the needs of Armenia and Karabagh. It does not take a doctorate to realize that this is not possible. The agenda of any government of Armenia or Karabagh, whatever its colors, will be set by the people of Armenia and Karabagh, well intentioned and warm speeches notwithstanding. And that is the way it should be.

When Diasporan political parties returned to Armenia between 1990 and 1991, they were already transformed by diasporization while, at the same time, they had determined some of the processes that had shaped the Diaspora. During those seventy years, the parties had adjusted and adapted as much as the communities had. It is true that their membership was made up of members of the community who were more "dedicated" to some values and goals. The parties decided, nonetheless, that they had a place in Armenia and Karabagh, that their ideologies and programs had a relevance to a people with whom they had had little to do for seven decades.

The decisions of the Diasporan parties to extend their presence to Armenia were neither self-evident nor inevitable. Diasporan parties could have decided that they had fulfilled their historic mission; they had assured that Diasporan existence had not lost its national and political dimensions; that the people of Armenia and Karabagh had devised their own processes for defining and pursuing agendas and for electing their leaders; they had created their own parties; and they had given rise to an independent Armenia. The rebirth of sovereign statehood was an excellent opportunity for the parties to reevaluate their missions. The three Diasporan parties decided, nonetheless, to establish branches in Armenia. The reason or reasons for those decisions remain as obscure as how these decisions were made.

Two comments, one related directly to this obscurity in decision making, deserve attention. Armenians in the Diaspora were used to the secretive deliberations of political parties. A remnant of the Ottoman predicament and continued in the early operational centers of the Near East, the secrecy of agendas, deliberations, internal elections, and decision making has been the norm for these parties, even in Western countries. Since 1990, the political parties of Armenia have held open party congresses, where policy debates and elections of party leaders are public events. For the people of independent and free Armenia, freed after seventy years of Communist party rule, secrecy was and remains suspect and untrustworthy.

But a more fundamental question—fundamental to the security, vital interests, and independence of Armenia as well as to the well-being of Diasporan communities—must be addressed, even if only hypothetically: the potential conflict of interest, when a Diasporan party that speaks for a Diasporan community also governs Armenia, and the vital interests of the host country and Armenia are in conflict. How would one party take responsibility for the defense of the vital interests of Armenia and/or Karabagh without, at the same time, creating serious problems for itself and for the different parts of the nation? What would give?

Patented answers based on the "imperative of oneness" will not do. Only in ideological constructs can such answers be satisfying. Ideologies distort realities for the sake of convenience and useless, even harmful, coherence. Only people who do not understand the predicament of Armenia and Karabagh, only those who are ignorant and proud of their ignorance can offer such answers and believe them to be satisfactory for all concerned. The question is also not that hypothetical. The dilemma arose in 1914, when the ARF spoke and negotiated on behalf of both segments of the Armenian people in the Ottoman and Russian empires, two states embarking on a war path. There are legitimate questions as to whether the ARF, or any other party in the same predicament, managed (or could have managed) that role very well.

The challenge of statehood for the Armenian Diaspora has been both painful and exhilarating. On a structural level, readjustments have been minimal. There has also not been an analysis of values, expectations, and performances. It is possible that just as it was used to idealizing Armenia, the Diaspora must also keep itself safe from analysis. That might work for the Diaspora, but it does not work for Armenia and Karabagh, especially if strategic calculations include the Diaspora, however defined, as a key ingredient in the making of foreign policy, economic development, and conflict resolution.

Describing the Diaspora as "eight million strong" and "wealthy" has conjured up images in Armenia and Karabagh that do not correspond to realities and that may inspire a false sense of security. Promising more than what one can deliver and not delivering what one promises are, in the face of history, irresponsible acts. Time will also determine whether, at the end, the expectations of the leaders of Armenia and Karabagh from this vibrant, hopeful, but otherwise difficult Diaspora are justified.

6.

Between Tragedies and Visions:
Will the Present Ever Arrive?

During the past decade, Armenians witnessed the rise of a popular movement that started with the demand for the unification of Karabagh and evolved quickly into a movement of national renewal. Under the leadership of the Karabagh Committee and then the Armenian National Movement (ANM), Armenia achieved independence, adopted political and economic reforms, and started building state institutions in the context of a new Constitution. Armenia overcame the immediate impact of blockades, resolved a serious energy crisis at least for the medium term, and was able to defend successfully Karabagh and its people while avoiding a wider war. It has one of the best armies in the former USSR space. And it has helped Karabagh to survive and develop its institutions, including a combat-ready army.

None of these achievements is perfect or can be taken for granted. Institutions are still fragile and being tested. They are functioning but must be consolidated. Reforms in the areas of justice, health care, education, and social security have been initiated but are far from being adequate or functional; they all require concentration, human and financial resources, and some imagination. There have been attempts to deal with corruption, yet a full war against it requires a substantial rise in the standard of living of all employees in the state sector, especially middle- and lower-level workers and bureaucrats. That, in turn, requires resources that the budget does not have and is not likely to have in the absence of peace.

Even though the downward trend in the economy was halted by 1994, economic growth is not assured and development has not yet produced a qualitative change in the standard of living for the majority of the population. Full recovery will require substantial and sustained foreign investment for which a safe and friendly environment is needed.

The ANM provided much of the leadership and political stamina for domestic changes as well as a new, nontraditional foreign policy. The leaders of the ANM assumed the positions of highest responsibility in state building and for the most part exhausted themselves, politically and physically. The party suffered from the fact that it was the party in power at a time of extremely trying conditions. The ANM also allowed itself to feel and display the arrogance of power and to be bloated with a large membership that did not necessarily share the party's basic philosophy.

Power and positions have a tendency either to chastise and humble individuals or to exaggerate their personal weaknesses. We have seen both. The new political culture lacked institutional safeguards and a vetting mechanism for civil and foreign service personnel. Under the circumstances, personalities became at least as important as institutions: Personal qualities and personality failures in leaders were immediately translated into institutional weaknesses and policy failures. Many individuals served well, along with thousands of non-affiliated government officials, administrators, and civil servants whose honesty and dedication have gone unrecognized in the rush to judgment. Others did not rise to the occasion; they failed to control personal ambitions and weaknesses. Some failed the President who appointed them as trusted colleagues.

The opposition parties often served as a check on excesses; on occasion they caused those excesses. Opposition or other, Armenia has many bright and talented politicians who have done and are still doing and giving their best. Yet the party system collectively and parties individually have failed to overcome the credibility gap, which was part of Soviet culture and was deepened by the trials and tribulations of the last decade. Parties and their leaders have failed to convince a cynical citizenry that they have the interests of the people at heart, or that their antagonisms are not merely battles for power and clashes of personalities.

Continuing shifts of party and personality alliances have reinforced the sense that it is power that matters, and not programs and policies. At the end, citizens make their choices on the basis of their sense of the personality of a candidate and what that personality evokes in them. Citizens of Armenia are circumspect; they like leaders who project balance and judgment. They do not trust extremes; they do not like ideologized discourse. And they like stability. That is the reason Robert Kocharian and Karen Demirjian, the former First Secretary of the Soviet Armenian Communist Party, received the highest number of votes in the 1998 presidential election. Both men projected poise, balance, circumspection, strength of personality, stability, and lack of ideologized discourse and vituperative rhetoric.

Beyond the meanderings of political parties and personalities, which is likely to continue, the central issue remains the Karabagh conflict. In Karabagh, Armenia's past, present, and future intersect. What we remember of history tells as much about our present and ourselves as it does about our past.

OF THE HISTORY OF WARS
AND THE WAR OF HISTORIES

History can be enslaving or liberating. It can be used as an aid to thinking or as a tool to achieve and retain power. It can be manipulated to legitimize one's prejudices and opinions or to break through mental structures and accepted wisdom. It can serve to comfort one by its familiarity, but it can also condemn a people to repeating the mistakes of the past.

Acquired historical wisdom has reduced the past into a series of decisions made by rulers who made moral choices to become heroes or martyrs. The history of the nation was reduced to the story of an individual; a person's personal choice ended up symbolizing a nation's political imperatives. In the process, the concept of "nation" has become an absolute value, set for all times, immutable. Some nations are good, others simply bad. Therefore, change in the current visualization of relations cannot occur.

Some historians share in this worldview and have reproduced it as scholarship. Post-Genocide national identity has often been projected into the very different contexts of the past.

Most Armenians who fell victim to the Genocide, for example, were peasants or small-town dwellers primarily because most Armenians were peasants and small-town dwellers, but also because the latter groups had fewer opportunities to escape or survive than did city dwellers. While historians do note the sorry lot of Armenians in the Eastern provinces, explanations of events are cast in the form of clashes of nationalities. What it meant for an Armenian peasant to be an Armenian in a village of Anatolia differed sharply, of course, not only from what it means for an Armenian to be in Moscow, Aleppo, or New York today, but also from what it meant then to have been an Armenian intellectual or an Armenian merchant in Istanbul or Tbilisi.

The self-image of the Armenian today, and the image he or she wants to project into host societies, is that of the urbanized, knowledgeable, educated, and professional Armenian—the civilized Armenian. A history of peasants does not make much sense today. Yet that projection into the past can succeed only at the expense of a useful history. Armenian peasants and small-town dwellers in the Eastern provinces were the root of the Armenian Question. They were the reason for the birth of the revolutionary parties. The collective lot of the rural Armenian population was also at the heart of the revolutionary parties: the Social Democratic Hunchakian Party (SDHP), but especially the Armenian Revolutionary Federation (ARF).

Beginning with its founding document of 1892, for example, the main constant in ARF programs was agrarian reform in the Eastern provinces of the Ottoman Empire, and after 1908 in the whole of the Empire. During the last substantial negotiations between the ARF and Young Turks from 1909 to 1911, before the latter decided on a policy of Genocide, the ARF started off with a long list of demands. The intransigence of the Young Turks compelled the ARF to narrow its demands to the bare minimum. For the ARF negotiators, the absolute minimum was agrarian reform, an extremely radical idea for the Young Turks, who had already abandoned the slogans of the 1908 Revolution and had adopted reactionary policies, in the economic as well as the political spheres.

The ARF reasoning could be relevant to the issues facing the nation today and might be instructive in any informed debate, whether about the past or for the future. The heartland of historic Armenia, the Eastern provinces of the Ottoman Empire, were being depopulated of their Armenian inhabitants. Massacres were only exacerbating emigration, not causing it. The real cause of emigration was the inability of the rural Armenians, townspeople and peasants, to ensure their economic survival. The European Industrial Revolution was producing goods and materials against which Armenian craftsmen could not compete. European imperialism and the Ottoman debt had, furthermore, compelled the Ottoman Empire to collect taxes in cash rather than in kind, when cash was hardly used in the rural, especially the peasant, population. Peasants could get cash only by ransoming their farms, and that was the end of the farm. The slow but steady emigration of the young and male population had left historic Armenia weak, its communal work force in shambles, its male population depleted. It is possible to argue that the economic dimension—the problem and its solution—are as much part of the story of the Genocide as is the ethnic dimension. The economic dimension made Genocide both desirable and possible for the Young Turks who, in addition to being Turkish nationalists, were social reactionaries. This explanation does not exhaust the motivations of the planners and perpetrators of the Genocide, but it does provide an example of the limitations and distortions to which our view of history is subject when we do not look critically at ourselves.

What will a long, drawn-out "no war but no peace" situation do to the population of Karabagh and Armenia, if there is no dramatic turn on the economic front?

At the end of one of our frequent discussions in Yerevan on possible options regarding OSCE Minsk Group proposals, a colleague once made a revealing pronouncement on our situation. He began by stating that he was not a historian himself, and he sounded as if he was proud of it. "I am told by someone who knows history," my colleague began, "that the problem in our history has been the diplomat who lost on the negotiating table what the soldier won on the battlefield."

I admitted to being, or having once been, a historian—no one was perfect, I said—and promised not to take unfair advantage of the difference. But I did point out that to my knowledge there have been few victories in the history of the Armenian people during the last one thousand years, not sufficient to make a generalization; that the victories have been in battles, not wars; and the confusion between a battle and a war has been costly; and that after any kind of victory, when there have been negotiations, the diplomat had lost not because he asked for too little, as my colleague was implying, but just possibly because he had asked for too much, more than he could swallow.

Battles do not create the long-term balance of power and interests that peace requires, and wars are not just a series of battles. While the outcome of a battle may be determined by the difference in the fighting spirit of the soldiers on the two sides of the trenches, wars are decided by long-term resources, strategic calculations, and allies, by the interests of other parties, whether engaged in the fighting or not. Battles can create status quos; even wars, nowadays, are unlikely to determine the ultimate outcome of a conflict.

My colleague's view was not surprising. He wanted very much to believe in the finality of the recent battlefield victories and their ability to dictate peace. This is an interpretation commonly adhered to by many Armenians, who, as a people, have a very long collective memory. But collective memory is often confused with knowledge of history. One example Armenians know is the victory of Russia over the Ottoman Empire in February 1878 and the subsequent Russian occupation of Ottoman or Western Armenian territories, enshrined in the Treaty of San Stefano with its famous Article 16 on reforms in the Armenian provinces. The problem was that the treaty was reversed when Great Britain threatened Russia with war. Russia withdrew, with all the dire consequences that Armenians then suffered.

My colleague's view was not surprising; but it was alarming. The surprising part was that many historians have frequently supported a similar logic. If it was not the diplomats, it was the "lack

of unity," "the immoral world,"—some "bottom-line," anyway—
that was at fault. But to draw a bottom-line lesson from the past
means accepting nothing less than what satisfies the absolute and
the maximum because everything else is a "piece of paper." Of
course, even if one receives the absolute and the maximum, they
still have to be consecrated and formalized on a "piece of paper,"
which can be torn and disregarded.

History is not a science; it cannot be repeated in a laboratory to
prove a hypothesis. But Armenians have had enough history to
understand critically and in its full complexity the world within
which they must make decisions, the environment within which
Armenia and Karabagh are functioning, and to assess what is to
change and what Armenians cannot change, however odious and
unfair reality may be. One should not have to go through another
calamity in order to prove that we have respect for the martyrs of
the first.

IDEOLOGY AND DIPLOMACY

At a recent seminar, I was asked about the different uses I had
made of the terms *national cause* and *nationalist cause*. The differences, I argued, were how the proponents of a given cause
define the perimeters of a problem and what they seek in its resolution. The approaches to the conflict of Nagorno Karabagh provide an excellent illustration. There are people who see the
conflict as a national cause, and others who claim it as a nationalist cause.

In both situations, one is dealing with a problem of national
significance, whether real or perceived. When viewed from the
perspective of a national cause, the problems are of the right of
the 150,000 Armenians currently living in Karabagh to live
securely and freely on a clearly demarcated and historically consecrated territory and also of the search for a way to achieve those
goals with the best security guarantees that can be obtained. The
Azerbaijani claim over the same territory and the international
recognition of the Azerbaijani claim make it necessary that Armenians deal with Azerbaijan and the international community to

find a solution acceptable to all concerned, a solution that will also preclude, as best possible, future threats.

When viewed from the nationalist perspective, the problem of Nagorno Karabagh is a manifestation of all that has gone wrong in the past and all that the future must be. Karabagh's woes represent all the losses Armenians have suffered through the centuries—territorial and otherwise. The people of Nagorno Karabagh and the territory itself constitute, within this perspective, the symbol of the injustices Armenians have suffered at the hands of the "Turks." Armenians there are vested with the task of changing the course of Armenian history. They are the living examples of the historic heroes and martyrs.

In the first case, Karabagh is the problem of real people, living today, in the world of today. In the second case the antagonist is Armenian history, or one's memory of it. In the first case, one tends to negotiate with the antagonist in order to resolve the problem. In the second, there is not much to negotiate; the "others" must give what one wants as a payment for the mistreatments and injustices of history. In the first case, one can accept a compromise based on the mutual recognition of legitimate concerns. In the second case, one tends to think of any compromise as treason to history, reduced to the memory of the people who died for the faith or the land.

Individuals who do not want to compromise and who want it all, including those who do not think diplomats and diplomacy serve a useful purpose, have an advantage: They give nothing away. They can don the garb of the patriot; they can accuse others of "selling" Karabagh. Most of all, they do not take responsibility in history, and if anything happens to Karabagh, they can always blame someone else—the immoral world and its ways, major powers and their games. A victim's psychology leaves one immune to responsibility. Then, bards will compose new songs to glorify the recently dead heroes and remember the innocent martyrs.

No Armenian political party, leader, or thinker has yet come up with a strategy to have it all—an independent Armenia that is also free and democratic, rich and without corruption and depravity; an Armenian Karabagh, and Karabagh-controlled occupied Azerbaijani territories. No one has yet figured out how to achieve all that while maintaining the eternal enmity of two of four neighbors and the love of the international community because of past victimization.

A historian once said that most conflicts in history are not resolved, they just become irrelevant. The history of Karabagh itself shows that when Armenians have not found the solution, someone else has imposed it and has made the conflict—and Armenians along with it—irrelevant, at least for a while.

A few words are in order regarding the question of strategies.

First, very little has changed in the level of morality of great, super, or major powers in the last few hundred years. Where there has been change, it is hardly relevant to Armenian concerns and to Karabagh. If the world was immoral, which in the view of some people explains the losses Armenians have suffered in history, it still is, and this fact should be taken for granted.

Second, it is not the business of other countries to like or dislike Armenia or Armenians, in Karabagh or elsewhere, as a state or as a minority. Armenians have to care for themselves. Major policy issues are not determined by love. No one should misinterpret sentiment in politics as an indication of what a country will or will not do regarding issues important to it.

Third, anti-Turkish reflexes transformed into ideology and masqueraded as diplomacy do not constitute a strategy, just as anti-Russian and pro-U.S. instincts do not. A belief that they do is the fastest way to lose the ability to define national interests, to surrender the freedom to think, and to become powers in someone else's game. Just because the antagonist accepts a solution and proposes one does not make that solution, ipso facto, unacceptable to Armenians; it may make it suspect, but not necessarily unacceptable.

What harms Turkey or Azerbaijan is not, by definition, good for Armenia or Karabagh. Embarrassing Turkey does not necessarily lead pro-Armenian and anti-Turkish allies to give, at the end, what one really wants. To spend all Armenian energies on embarrassing Turkey or Azerbaijan is a waste of time. Both do a very good job of that on their own, and if more is needed, let pro-Armenian friends do it. They have many more resources. In some instances, Armenians have to speak up, but these instances have to be decided by Armenians, case by case, in the context of Armenians' own interests and strategy.

Fourth, a statement of one's dreams and goals does not amount to a strategy, and a more forceful assertion of dreams and goals does not bring a statement closer to becoming a strategy. Certainly listing one's sufferings does not make an argument more convincing.

Fifth, the purpose of a strategy is not to gain new arguments that prove one's moral superiority, the purity of one's ideology, the crassness of others, the legitimization of one's comfort with the psychology of a victim, or the chance for new martyrdom.

Sixth, a thousand clever tactical steps do not amount to a strategy, unless one knows where they are leading and how they fit in the strategies and goals of others.

The test of a good strategy is its success. The test of good diplomacy is obtaining the minimum one needs and the maximum one can get. Nothing more, nothing less.

Making a spectrum of choices possible is the greatness of the soldier. Determining the national interest is the test of the leader's statesmanship. Ensuring that the national interest is secured and reaching out to the maximum is the job of the diplomat. All in a real, untidy, and an uncertain world. The ideologue's role is to complain about events that do not fit neatly into his or her favorite pattern or model of a sanitized world, unless, of course, the ideologue comes to power, in which case he or she either becomes a statesman or diplomat, or becomes irrelevant to the solution of the problem and makes the problem irrelevant by causing a calamity.

A strategy begins with the right calculation of the relation among forces—military, political, diplomatic, financial, and economic—now and in the future, within the regional and international environment, and with any realistic prospect of changing them. A good strategy eliminates wishful thinking, vague hopes for more favorable conditions, risks one cannot take, and ideological distortions.

CHOOSING THE RIGHT MOMENT

A good strategy includes the choice of the right moment when you have the best hand to make a deal. Identifying that moment is one of the more difficult tasks of the leader-stateperson. The moment has much less to do with some of the specifics of any given proposal as the basis of negotiations than with the political will that a deal must be made. And a deal requires more than one party to the conflict.

The question is whether, at the end, the Armenian side has already missed or will miss that moment. The Party of Karabagh, wavering between seeing Karabagh as a national cause and a nationalist cause, determined that Ter-Petrossian's choice of moment was not the right one. One can hear whispers from within the group that no moment is the right moment. But so far Kocharian has avoided ideological trappings, although he believes he can use ideology as another weapon for very pragmatic purposes.

Kocharian may have been right; he may succeed in implementing his project, and find a better moment. It is possible that economic growth will occur on a scale that brings about a qualitative change in the lives of Armenians and Karabagh, that the balance of power is maintained without resorting to a new round of fighting, and that the bases for Azerbaijan's optimism about its future are so weakened that it will be compelled to give Karabagh and Armenia all they want. Unlikely scenario, but a possible one.

But for that scenario to have a chance for success, Armenians in Armenia, in Karabagh, and in the Diaspora—as leaders, as organizations, as parties—must give this scenario a chance. Particular responsibility rests on the shoulders of those who rejected every opportunity for peace presented thus far and who worked hard to undermine Ter-Petrossian's position and policies. They convinced Kocharian that his interpretation of the situation was correct and encouraged his line on Karabagh. For that scenario to succeed, the President must be given a chance so he can avoid spending his time and energy on petty politics and can escape the hold of ideologically induced paralysis. Ter-Petrossian did want to give him that chance by attending the presidential inauguration of the man who forced his resignation. Subsequently, Ter-Petrossian stated that he was open to cooperation, despite his deep differences with the new President. When I met Kocharian in Yerevan in April 1998, I communicated my readiness to assist in any way I could, despite my deep disagreement with his actions and analyses. That has not been the case with those on whom Kocharian relied when he assumed the leadership. The reality of statehood does not seem to have challenged everyone to rethink and reevaluate positions and priorities.

Another possibility is that Kocharian was wrong and will not be able to get the results he expects. He may find that unity meant different things to different politicians and leaders, that claiming an ideology, including a national ideology, is not the same as idealized behavior. In this case, he will either attempt a pragmatic solution or turn to the ideologists for cover. But they would not trust the implementation of their visions to an eclectic. The prospects of competing ideologies seeking control of power is too horrible to contemplate, but ideologies tend to turn politics into battlefields.

At that point, regardless of who is in power in a completely exhausted Armenia, the questions will be: Which of the nationalistic or ideological parties in power will have to run for a deal, any deal. In other words, the question will be: Which of the countries on whom Armenia and Karabagh will have come to depend for mere survival will be selling Karabagh to Azerbaijan? Then the Armenian side will have little to say about the conditions of sale.

Some people may find this a pessimistic, even defeatist scenario. Whatever the characterization, Armenian history suggests that such a scenario has happened before. Armenian history and the history of other nations and conflicts suggest that military or diplomatic strategy based on the most optimistic and questionable projections are, at best, risky business, and at worst, a recipe for disaster.

The resolution of the conflict must remain a priority for a number of reasons. Conflicts sometimes impose their own logic on a situation. So much has been invested by so many domestic and international forces in that conflict—some favoring resolution and others pushing in the direction of nonresolution—that the question of war or peace may be the more immediate one. It may be possible to preserve the status quo for a while, but military logic will most likely prevail again, unless a peace treaty appears in the horizon. Even keeping the status quo and the present balance of power may dictate a new round of fighting. Both parties, the Azerbaijani and the Armenian side, may believe time is on their side. Both are wrong. Both may at the end lose much more than the points of disagreement that constitute obstacles to a peace agreement today. The fact that Azerbaijan too is miscalculating and has much to lose should not be a source of consolation to any Armenian, if in the process the Armenian side loses as well—and loses something that cannot be recovered.

Armenians must realize that the unresolved conflict has been eating away at the body politic and has been eroding the foundations of society, all idealizations and ideologies notwithstanding. No nation escapes the economic costs of war. Beyond defense budgets, wars have hidden costs to the economy. No nation escapes the political costs of war. Unable to address the real issue, politicians distort their logic and program to deal with issues as if the conflict did not exist. They hide their policies and fall into exaggerations and extremes. Their discourse hides more than it reveals.

In addition, the arms race will weaken Armenia's balanced foreign policy as it increases its dependence on one or two countries, particularly when increasing pressures from ideologically motivated groups have already pushed policy makers under Kocharian to feel uncomfortable with an international environment that no longer represents clear, divided camps.

No nation escapes the moral costs of war. Unable to address the need for a speedy solution lest they be charged with treason and defeatism, citizens and groups vent their anger in ways that weaken traditional values and bonds, social cohesion, and analytical ability. Anger turns against Karabaghtsis and each other. Festering conflicts deepen existing chasms and create new ones. Prejudices turn into resentment and become legitimate points of view. Unity becomes even more elusive.

The prospect of living in eternal enmity with two of one's four neighbors is not and should not be an option, regardless of the ideology that such a situation would serve. The more the stale-mate continues, the more difficult it becomes to part with occu-pied territories unnecessary to Armenian security. Occupied territories, which once were guarantees of security, turn into the most serious source of insecurity. A solution that does not consider the legitimate interests of the antagonist will not be a lasting solution. Can Armenians learn to manage victory as well as tragedy?

Finally, for a century now, since the robe of modern national-ism was placed on the Armenian people with the promise of sal-vation, Armenians have been living with the hope that someday they could exercise their right to live—and to live in dignity. Armenians know what World War I cost them. Throughout the Soviet period the people in Armenia and Karabagh lived for the future. In the name of an ideology that promised a better future they gave up their present. In the name of an ideology they were asked to sacrifice their freedoms, theirs options, and their dignity.

The present should finally arrive for the people of Armenia and Karabagh. Armenians there have the right to expect a decent education for their children, adequate health care, a secure retire-ment; they have the right to a happier life that Diasporans have secured by becoming and remaining a Diaspora. Armenians in the Diaspora or, for that matter, political elites anywhere should not expect the people of Armenia and Karabagh to sacrifice, once more, their lives and their present to ensure the realization of the dreams and visions of grandeur of others.

The battle being waged today is the battle between the search for normalcy based on pragmatic concerns and ideologically dri-ven visions of grandeur; it is being waged in the name of Karabagh and Armenia and the Armenian nation and, I hope, not at their expense.